Mental Models Tools

Great Techniques to Upgrade Your Thinking Skills and Achieve Super Performance. Tips, and Tricks to Improve Your Critical Thinking, Problem Solving, and Decision-Making Process

By

Brandon Dark

Table of Contents

Introduction

Congratulations on taking the next step to have the life you have always wanted! *Mental Models Tools* will help you understand what they are and how they can increase your productivity. In the following chapters, you will find tips and actions you can take right now to help you move closer to the life you want.

This book will not only explain what mental models are but, how they can work in your everyday and business life. Easy step-by-step actions that you can take to get started on changing your mental models into more positive and productive models. These models will take you to the next level in your life and business.

It will teach you to become more goal orientated and focused on getting what you want out of life and business. Metal Models Tools will help you be more organized in your thinking so, you can get more accomplished.

It is understanding that when you learn these mental model tools, you can teach your business team to do the same. In turn, your business will be a team because everyone will know the goal of the company, and everyone will have a voice and will feel a part of the more significant cause.

You will have a history of mental models and the brilliant scientist that has brought this concept to so many people.

In business, when you allow the employees to grow as a person that growth shows up in their work-life as well. It is a winning situation. Understanding this element will increase the lives of the employee and the company as a whole.

Mental models are different for everyone. No two people think alike all the time. Our experiences, education, upbringing, and everything else that has happened in our life shape our mental models. Some of these, have not always had a positive outcome. This is where we can change them, and this book will help you do it.

Chapter 1: What Are the Mental Models?

The definition of the term mental models is explained in Wikipedia as followed "A mental model is an explanation of someone's thought process about how something works in the real world. It is a representation of the surrounding world, the relationships between its various parts, and a person's intuitive perception about his or her acts and their consequences."

Each person sees the world differently. No two people think alike on everything. The reason is because of all that our brains have taken in over the years. Education, experiences (good and bad), religion, our parents, and family. Everything in our life that has molded us into what we are today. We have specific patterns we use to problem solve. We both could come up with the same answer on a mathematical problem but, how we both had gotten that answer could have been different. The outcome was the same, but the methods were very different. The thinking patterns between senior adults and teenagers, children and parents, females and males are different. Most of us have already established this difference by this point in our lives.

The good thing about this is we all bring different perspectives to the table. Which, in turn, we can come up with a solution to the problem at hand. Having different views on the issue will open your eyes (and others) to see things differently but, yet still have your perspective on it but, in a different way. You are looking at it differently as well.

For example, there are 10 acres of flat land with a pond. The realtor sees profit in selling it, and a developer sees high rise buildings, the environmentalist sees how this land could be preserved and help flourish. A biologist sees ways to protect the animals and all living things on this property. It is the same land but many different views on what to do with it. It doesn't mean one is right, and one is wrong; it only means they are different.

These different views and perspectives also bring the opportunity to open your mind to different ways of thinking or viewing things. If your brain thinks more critically, then, having a creative mind on the team project may open your mind up to new ways of thinking just as your thinking will open the way they think. The ideas will flow both ways for everyone. Having more than one person working on a project brings more ideas on how to solve the problem or situation that the team is facing.

The decisions we make are based on what we have experienced in our lives or what we believe to be true. We use mental models to survive, create, improve on what is already here. Thousands and thousands of models are in our system. Some of these models we don't realize we even have them or use them. Mental models are based on experiences, intuitive, religion, childhood, health everything! Mental models are everything we think about and do.

Some may not consider intuition as part of your mental models, but it is included. Intuition is a feeling you get but, can't explain and really don't need to "think" the situation through. It is the gut feeling people talk about having. The feeling you have as a teenager when you know you shouldn't be at this party but, you went anyway, and the cops showed up, and you keep thinking "I knew I shouldn't have come. I should have listened to my gut." Yep, that is intuition. Intuition gives you insights on not only how to survive but, also how to create and bring your life to the next level. A voice tells you to take a break from writing your book and take your dog for a walk, and you listen to that voice and take the dog for a walk.

In doing so, you bump into the man of your dreams. That urge to tell your idea to everyone sitting in the board room and you don't know why. The thought you have about talking to that stranger but, you have no idea why and then find out they are just the person you need for your business. The intuition works for all of us, all the time. We have to listen; we have to act upon what it is telling us. We may not understand at the time, but it will show why that action needed to be done eventually.

Intuition is called a lot of different names. God, Universe, Holy Spirit, Great Divine, Inner Self. Whatever you call it, listen to it, and listen to it often. It will lead you in the right direction. It may not be the direction you "THINK" you should be going in but, trust your gut; it knows where you need to be at all times.

The Historic People Behind Mental Models:

Kenneth Craik (Philosopher and Psychologist)

A philosopher and psychologist by the name of Kenneth Craik was born in Scotland and studied extensively in Scotland as well as England. At the University of Edinburgh, he had studied philosophy. He also earned his doctorate from Cambridge University in 1940. Fellowship was at St. John's College, Cambridge in 1941. He had written a book (essay) in 1943 called "The nature of explanation." This book (essay) was the first to mention the term "mental models" though, it is unclear of the origin of the term but, he was the first one to bring it to light. The book is still a big part of studies done all around the globe. Some argue, and some agree with the ideas he had in this book.

This book was written right before the impact of digital computers.   Kenneth Craik took the concept (perspective) as the mind is a very complex machine. He is using symbolism that is used in machinal devices the same way as how our thought process works.   After coming up with this concept, he asked himself why? Why is an explanation sought after in the first place? In conclusion, it was a way to adapt to our world or surroundings. Our future looks at what we need to change or do to come up with a solution.

If a hurricane is coming to the coast and you live on that coastline. You want to know as much as you can about the storm so you can prepare your home and self for whatever it brings. Is it strong? How strong? Is it bad enough for me to leave the area? Can I stay and wait it out? We start to calculate and determine "what if" happenings. We want to evaluate the situation and try to "figure out" what our next moves will be. Predictions that are calculated and determined for the future. Some models are for our survival.

Flight or fight scenario plays a part in this situation also again, another mental model. It takes several models to make one decision. It never really is one thought or way of thinking. It is several ways of thinking. In this situation, you are using a fight or flight, should I stay or go? Calculating how much time you have before it hits, what will you need for the trip out of the area and when you should leave and how far away you should go. So, mathematics plays a part in it too. I have been in this situation before, what happened the last time? The memory of having to do this before. Different models are firing at the same time to help you figure the problem out.

In World War II he had been a part of a team, along with Gordon Butler Iles that had dramatic advances on the flight simulators for the RAF (The Royal Air Force). Along with these advances, they also did extensive studies on the lack of sleep in pilots and what effects it had on them. His work has helped many studies in cognitive science.   He had opened a door for so many advancements.   Kenneth Craik was killed only a few years after writing "The nature of explanation." He was hit by a car as he was riding his bicycle, he was taken to the hospital and died the next day. In his short career, he has raised awareness of the mental models and the new age of cybernetics. He indeed was a pioneer in this field of mental models.

Philip Johnson-Laird (Professor and Author)

Philip Johnson-Laird was born in 1936 in Leeds, United Kingdom. Philip Johnson-Laird was doing odd jobs for ten years before he decided to head to school and become a professor and earning his Ph.D. in 1967. It is never too late to start. I think what I like about his work most is that his writing is easy to understand. A degree in science or psychology to understand what he is explaining is not necessary. Kenneth Craik, on the other hand, it would be helpful.

There are so many areas of the human thought process that are studied and how mental models play a role in all of them. Dr. Johnson-Laird has written many books on the human reasoning mental models. Mental models are the thoughts we have. The ideas we have and putting them together to create a plan to solve a problem we have at hand. It could be as simple as getting across a busy street and as complex as learning calculus in college. The field of reasoning that Philip studied and wrote about was how we make decisions and the reasoning we put behind them.

We could make a wise decision and be it be an amazing one or make a wrong decision and have a horrible outcome. Either way, the reasoning behind it is based on our mental models. He points out limiting beliefs are a massive part of why we continue to make bad decisions. We can't "see" the possibilities that will come out of a particular decision. We only see what our memories have shown us. So, in turn, we limit the beliefs and continue to think we can't do something because it didn't work in the past.

A woman considers leaving an abusive relationship. Her rational thoughts (mental models) tells her she should go and never come back. That, this behavior is not healthy for a person on so many levels, physical and mental. This would be the right decision and would lead to a healthier, happier lifestyle and could open one's life up to numerous positive opportunities. The woman had tried to leave previously, and the abuser has beat her so severely she was admitted to the hospital. The limiting beliefs and memories keep her in the relationship. She cannot see the possibilities leaving the relationship would hold for her because she only can see the past. So, she will tell herself "stories" (mental models) to stay and convince herself that it is the best move for her. She will make excuses for her abuser and tell herself he loves her. He is just having a hard time and is stressed about work. He will be kind to her and show attention, and this will reinforce what she is telling herself. When her abuser attacks again, she will blame it on the drinking he has done all day. She will use the reason even when the idea doesn't make sense.

The reasoning is a lie, and she will convince herself it is true. Her mental models are based on memories and blurred to the possibilities leaving would hold for her. It doesn't matter what anyone else says. She will continue to stay until SHE changes the mental models. Once you learn something good or bad, it is hard to change it. Once, you decide to improve your mental models to a more successful outcome, and you won't go back to the way they were. You have made new connections and will have different mental models that will serve you better.

Dr. Philip Johnson-Laird studied at the University of London and received his Ph.D. there. He also had won the International Prize which an award presented to a candidate that had distinguished research in an area supported by the foundation. He had taught at Princeton University and was a senior scholar of the department of psychology. He also received an honorary doctor in science degree from Princeton in 1996. He retired in 2012 after 23 years of teaching. He has done outstanding work on reasoning and language learning.

Ruth M. J. Byrne (Cognitive Scientist and Author)

Ruth Byrne had attended Trinity College Dublin and the University College Dublin. She is now a cognitive science professor at the Trinity College of Dublin. She is an author of several books and essays regarding the imagination. The study of imagination is not one that has been studied a lot. But, in her book "The Rational Imagination" she brings to our attention how imagination thinking is linked to rational thinking more closely than previously thought.

The guidelines that we use for rational thinking is also used in imaginative thinking. The difference between the two is with imagination thinking or creative thinking; we are solving a problem with new ideas a new way of thinking that has no limits. It is free to wonder any way to solve the problem. Whereas, rational thinking is based on the information and facts that are available at the time. It is a more limited way of thinking because we only have the information that is given or facts. Ruth

Byrne thinks that these two ways of thinking are similar in how we process it.

We still observe, analysis and solve the problem but, just in different ways. Critical thinking, for example, is when a contractor looks at a blueprint of a house and has to figure out how much lumber is needed to frame the house, build walls, staircase, etc. A creative thinker is bringing new ideas to the world. The creative thinker has a way of looking at the same problem but, finding new ways to figure them out. They are "out of the box" thinkers. They don't see it like everyone else. A fashion designer that is creating a new line of clothes for a casual work look, most fashion designers don't do that. They could use colors, fabric, patterns in different ways to create the look they have in their minds. The mind is open to new ideas.

Dr. Ruth Byrne has also studied counterfactual thoughts or counterfactual mental models. It is the concept of creating an alternate outcome of a past situation. The "if only" or "what If." If Mary had taken her usual routine to work, she wouldn't be in an accident. The way the mind thinks about past situations and imagine what we could have done differently. If Tom would have said he loved Sara, they would still be together. What if Stacie was voted class president. At some point, the mind will take these "what if" and make them part of the history even if it wasn't what really happened.

We wanted the "what if" to be true that the mind starts to believe it. We all perceive a situation differently and looking back on that situation years later may even produce a different idea of what happened at the time. All concepts of thinking are needed to guide us and help us make the right decisions and move us forward to a better life. All of these ideas and concepts will help shape the new generation of thinkers. They will add to what is already here and create the next level of information and studies.

Peter Senge (American System Scientist, Author)

Peter Senge has been an enormous influence on the way businesses are run today. He has written several books on system thinking. The one that has changed the business world the most has been "The fifth discipline." This book gives the groundwork to have a successful business by using the organization and system thinking structure. The concept behind this is to include everyone in the company from the least paid to the most paid. Everyone's ideas count, and everyone works together as a team. The team concept is the framework for the new way business is done.

Peter Senge is a pioneer in the learning Organization thinking. Peter is a graduate from MIT and now is the senior lecturer there. Peter has created a system for both the company and the employee to grow and expand together as well as individually. Organization and system thinking are vital to creating a successful business that will withstand the years. Helping the employee become a better person and have a more positive perspective on life will not only enhance that employee, but it will also benefit the company.

Happy employees are more efficient and will create results in problems. If an employee feels she can express ideas and be creative in a safe work environment, she is more likely to speak up and give significant input. If an employee feels a sense of belonging and that their ideas will be heard in a safe and open work environment, more creative concepts to resolve problems will come forth. In his book "The Fifth Discipline," he explains the five principles to create a learning organization system. We will examine each and give an example to understand better how the system works.

Build a Shared Vision

Create a vision for the company that everyone can feel they had a part in it. Ask employees their opinion and make them a part of the vision. Employees want to do a task because they are asked not because they are told by management. If everyone in the company has the same CLEAR vision, the flow of the business will be smoother because everyone is working towards the same goal or vision.

If a company's vision is to help children with learning disabilities to learn easier. This vision should be on everyone's mind when creating or doing daily business. From customer service to the researchers gathering information for a new program. They all have to be on the same page and work together to uphold that vision. If the mental models are all the same throughout the company, then, the company and employees will work together as a team.

A vision should excite the whole company. Whether it is six employees or 6,000. It has to be something that they can get behind and believe in. Having a sense of common ground can help grow a business in the right direction. A shared vision is a vision everyone can support. That is the glue to keep the company growing and going.

System Thinking

System thinking is the process of looking at a company as a whole. Looking at how each department affects another and how the employees in each of those departments affect each other. How a company works together is an essential key to running a smooth and successful operation. Employees look at each other, not as rivals but, as team members. All on one team striving for the same goal. If the company has a vision that the employees can believe in, then that is a recipe for success.

Each employee in each department will help the company strive to new heights by understanding it is all about the teamwork. Teamwork within the department and teamwork within the company. Teamwork is what makes the dream work. It doesn't matter how big or how small the company.

This concept will carry the company far. Another critical factor in system thinking is to improve the employee as an individual. Help them grow, expand, gain knowledge, and this attitude will spill over into the work-life as well as personal life. That makes for a happy employee which in turn will be loyal and productive in the workplace. Trust and understanding from both employee and management create an open and honest environment that will strengthen over the years.

Mental Models in Business

Mental models are thoughts. A way of thinking and making sense of the world. A certain way you do things. What was learned as a kid or beliefs that have been developed over time. In the business world, mental models can determine how a company will stay in business or end up failing. The models have to change with the times. They can't stay the same because the world is always changing, and the company has to change with the times in order to stay in business. Old mental models can only get the company so far.

A past mental model for a company could be that they aren't willing to advertise on social media of any kind. Business experts know that social media is a perfect inexpensive way to reach new clients or customers. So, this mental model wouldn't serve the company well and could cost them a lot of business. If the advertising department came together and created for the social media platforms, the company would see the positive results that social media would have for them. They would have to be willing to change the mental model in order to reap the benefits.

Mental models can change throughout a company's life, but the vision should be the same, just a different way to think about what the company wants. Even when a company decided to go in a new direction (this is a mental model) they changed how they see the company and made an adjustment.

Mental models for the company should be expressed with all the employees of that company. This way, everyone is on the same path to reach the goal of the company. The best way a company can grow and expand in a new positive habit is by shifting and adapting to new mental models. A company can succeed; it has to be willing to be flexible. Understand adopting new mental models and seeking new, more efficient ways of doing business will only make it a better company that will last for years.

Growing and learning to expand as individuals, as well as a company only spells success. The world of business is always changing, and the company has to be ready and willing to grow and change with it. This is where new mental model changes can happen. Willing to change the way it operates to accommodate change is a way to last for many years to come.

Here is an example of mental models in business. If sales are down in a company, the company will research why this is happening. The data is in, and the company sees the sales have been down the last two months. The company decides to have a meeting with all the salespeople. In a company that practices organization systems, no "finger-pointing" or shaming will commence. The company will state the fact of what the reports are showing. That would be that sales are down. The company will then ask if anyone has a suggestion or think of why the problem exists. The salespeople think, and one young lady informs the company that the way they are contacting potential clients seems awkward and so unfriendly.

The company asks for ideas to change the problem and find a solution that everyone can benefit from. One by one, the sales team suggests and comes up with a new sales plan (mental model change) to contact more clients without feeling so awkward. The sales team comes up with a new mental model, and they all feel good about the change. The next month the sales had doubled from previous months. Problem solved, and everyone had a say so in the change. By coming together, the sales team (team members and management) solved the problem and constructed new ways of doing business. New mental models.

Team Learning in Business

Team learning can be used just about anywhere in life when more than one person is working on the same project. But, for now, we will talk about it in the business aspect. Team learning is taking knowledge of personal mastery and infusing it with a shared vision. It is the connecting point of the two. This is what I mean. When an employee can think of her co-workers as team members and not view them as a rival. Thinking of others as being on the same team and having the same vision (company vision) creates a teamwork environment that will build and grow a company instead of cause frustration and conflict within the company. This teamwork doesn't just happen in a company; the company creates it.

The company structures the environment as a safe and open one without judgment or punishment for mistakes. In turn, all the employees feel free to express their concerns and ideas and creates a bond that will help everyone succeed. Having this team concept helps the employees take more healthy risks because the team will succeed or fail together. It is easier to do that in a group than by oneself. Each employee will bring different strengths to the group.

Employees will work together and bring out the strengths of each other. Sara may be great at creating, and Bob could be great at organizing and spreadsheets. Bringing these two together will help boost confidence and trust between them because they depend on each other and support each other.

Teamwork will build trust in the employees and will build confidence in the company. The employee will be loyal to the company if the company believes in them, and respect and trust are instilled throughout the company.

When the market crashed, and business was way down, the company provided work for the employees and paid them for a 40-hour workweek. In conclusion to this, they were not laying any one-off. This created trust and loyalty to the company from the employees. The employees felt as if the company valued them and in turn, the employees will be more willing to help the company in the future.

Personal Mastery

Personal Mastery is a system of training. You are training to be a better you. Meaning you will expand your life skills by creating disciplines that will help you change the mental models that are not serving you. If the mental model you believe the claim, you are not smart enough to go back to school and be a nurse lIke you have always wanted to be. Having a family, a full-time job, and going to school seems so overwhelming and impossible to do.

The mental model you have created for yourself believes you have to stay where you are in the comfort zone. New positive mental models tell you it can happen. You stayed disciplined in the new system you have created for yourself. So, you start to believe this new mental model.

Over the next few years, you earn your degree, and now you are working full time in a doctor's office and enjoying the benefits of doing what you love, financial security, and spending more time with your family. Changing mental models can be scary at first but, keep moving forward, and you will see it will bring you a better, more satisfying life.

Create disciplines that advance your knowledge and opens your mind to a different, more positive perspective. Meditation, journaling, listening to positive podcasts, reading self-help books, and finding tips to improve your life is part of personal mastery. Mastering yourself, be in control of your own joy and happiness. Controlling what you can and letting go of what you can't control. Find peace with your life; this is personal mastery.

Tammy wanted to find a way to easy her chattering mind through the day. She found an article that meditation every day for 15 minutes would help control your monkey brain. It will give you a sense of peace. Desperate to try anything, she found an app on her phone, and each day she would meditate for 15 minutes in the morning. It was hard at first, and she felt like giving up but, wanting to control her thoughts, she kept going (creating a new mental model).

Within, a few months, she found herself at ease and peace throughout the day, and her mind seemed quieter. At night she was able to sleep because her mind wasn't racing with monkey thoughts. She created a new mental model, and life became better. Keep going it will change, give it time.

Peter Senge and his colleagues had a significant impact on the way businesses are currently operated. His own personal mastery helped develop the tools needed for an open organization system. This system helps everyone grow and expand to be better people and a better company.

Chapter 2: Creating Mental Models That Will Enhance Your Daily Life

Mental models are created by the experiences we have with family, school, and friends. Everything in your life shapes your mental models. When you were eight years old and was bitten by the neighbor's big dog? This mental model was created that all big dogs were going to bite you or be aggressive. It is a false mental model, but your mind believes it. So, it is true for you.

The mental model can be changed, as well. You could start by visiting friends with big dogs that are gentle giants. Be in the same room and start to pet and interact with them. Keep doing this until your brain makes new mental model connections. Connections that support that not all big dogs are aggressive and will bite you. Once, you are comfortable with the idea of being around big dogs, your anxiety will reduce, and you will feel at ease around a bigger breed of dogs. The new mental model you will have is that not all big dogs are aggressive.

Negative thoughts come to us humans naturally and easily. Dating all the way back to caveman days. Our ancestors were always worrying about being eaten. They were always on the lookout for predators. They focused on the worst things that could happen because well, at that time, the worst usually did happen. They were always in survival mental models. It is in our DNA to think the worst! We find it easier to complain and stress and worry instead of just being happy and content. We can, but at times, we let the negative take over.

A negative mental model would view this scenario like this. You are in a fender bender, leaving the grocery store. Not a big deal but, just an inconvenience at the time. Two days later you drop your new phone and the screen cracks on it. Today you forgot your lunch on the counter this morning and had to walk to the cafeteria to have lunch. A negative attitude would complain and ask why are these terrible experiences are happing to me? They would dwell on the negative and negative things will continue to happen as long as the negative mental models are still in place.

On a positive attitude, the person would think well; the accident could have been a lot worse. I could have been without a car for several weeks. The phone screen could have been cracked so bad I couldn't have used it, but it wasn't. Walking to the cafeteria will help me get my steps in for the day. Can you see the difference between the two? Having a positive mental model will create a more satisfying and grateful life. WHY? You will be thankful for the situation that it wasn't worse. You will feel happy and joy more during the day and the rest of your life.

The key to creating new mental models are recognizing the old ones that are not serving you. The ones that restrict you from getting out of your comfort zone or not letting you be the best version of yourself. Once, these mental models have been brought to your attention; you can start to change them and create mental models that will enhance your life. Getting exercise in for 20 to 30 minutes a day will increase your health. This will also help with information processing, release stress, and help create new mental model connections.

If you are faced with a problem and it is troubling you, consider going for a walk or run. Exercising could give you the answer you are looking for. You and your best friend have had a huge argument, and you have been feeling stressed all day about it and not sure what to do.

You CHOOSE to take a run and start to think of the conversation, and while you are running, you begin to make new mental model connections. You begin to look at the argument differently and can see her side of the dilemma. After the run, you feel better. Your mind is clear, and your body feels relief because you have just released all the stress that you have had all day.

The choice to make new, better mental models is up to us. We can keep living the way we are, not do anything differently and inside feel miserable and unfulfilled or choose to be happy and joyful. The choice is always up to you. We can choose to be happy or sad. So, choose wisely.

The comfort zone is where safety and security are felt even if we are miserable and unhappy with our life. The world around us is always changing, and we have to change with it. Staying in the comfort zone will not continue to serve you. You want to lose forty pounds, but you are scared to go to the gym because you think others will criticize you.

So, you let the feeling of insecurity and rejection keep you from getting healthy and feeling better. This is how a comfort zone can keep you from being a better version of yourself. The flip side of that is, or creating new mental models, is if you did decide to go to the gym 3 days a week and take advantage of the personal trainer the gym offers you will shed the forty pounds (if not more) and feel strong, confident and more positive and willing to try new things and make new mental model connections. You will start to expand your learning and self-care along with wanting to help others in ways that feel good to you.

All this newfound beautiful life by stepping out of the comfort zone and creating new mental models. In order for humans to be the best version of themselves, they have to keep moving out of the comfort zone. New mental models also, means new comfort zones. Recognizing the comfort zones will keep you moving forward and experiencing all that life has to offer you. Keep moving; you will keep improving yourself when you do. Most of the time, we are simply scared to move out of that comfort zone. We fear failure, rejection, or being singled out.

We all want to "fit in" we are a gathering species. It's what we do. We like the connection to our tribe, and sometimes we go against what our inner mental models tell us and do what we feel we have to do to stay in the tribe. What isn't realized is when you follow your true mental models that serve you well? You will find your TRUE tribe, and it will be amazing! Be willing to create new mental models and be open to new people that may turn out to be your new tribe that will accept your uniqueness because they will have similar mental models that align with yours. Be brave to discover new mental model connections.

A positive mental model can benefit you in so many ways. Changing them at times can be challenging, and other times it will be simple. It will take time to create these new mental models that will serve your life. So, don't give up if you don't see results with some of them right away. Meditation will seem hard for some because we are not always able to sit quietly and to listen to our inner guide. The world around us is always busy. Lots of noise and going places are happening. Sitting still is uncomfortable and hard for some of us.

The more we do it and do it daily, the easier it will get. It may take months to feel the benefits, but they will come just keep working at it. Other changes will come easily, like brushing your teeth with your non-dominant hand. Sounds silly but, it makes your brain think differently. Creating new mental models, maybe this will give you an idea you haven't considered before by brushing your teeth with the dominant hand. Simple changes in mental models can bring HUGE inspiration. A new perspective on how to see the world and how you function in the world.

How a Positive Outlook Can Change Your Situation

Think of all the positive people in your life. No matter if the situation is good or bad, they always have a positive attitude even on horrible days. The mind is a powerful tool. Mental models can make life harder or easier. The choice is yours. Taking responsibility for your actions and your choices in your life and admitting when you are wrong are huge steps to a more fulfilling life. Changing mental models and consistency can help you create a habit that will be rewarding throughout your life.

Start to understand yourself. You recognize negative mental models and start to look at where they started and why they started. Ask yourself if that mental model is serving you now. If not, change that mental model. It will take time, but, the next time this issue comes up, you will know what to do. The beautiful thing is you can change them. You can make new connections and love yourself more.

When friends argue, you always step in and try to help calm everyone down. You have always done it as long as you can remember but, doing this always brings you in the middle of the drama when the drama really isn't yours. You feel stressed, anxious, and sad long after it is over. You start to look at this more closely and realize you did this when your parents fought when you were a child.

A mental model you formed to calm everyone down at the expense of yourself. It wasn't your place to calm everyone down, and it still isn't. Letting people figure out their own arguments is what you need to let happen. You don't have to keep peace with everyone anymore. This mental model does not serve you anymore. Change it.

Being overweight is hard but, so is getting healthy. What hard do you want to deal with more overweight hard or getting healthy hard?

Personal Mental Model Shifts to Be More Sufficient

Discover what mental models are working for you. Use those more. A great way to start your mental model change is to exercise. Not only will it help your body but, it will also improve your mind. When our bodies are in motion, we are releasing stress from our brain and our body. Our mood is better. We can begin to think clearly. Exercise does so much for the mind and body. Eating healthy foods can also boost brainpower. Our body needs fuel to function properly right along with our brain. Not just food like fast food, or junk food but, real food like veggies, fruits, whole grains, lean meats. If we eat more of the good stuff and limit the not so good stuff, we will feel and function so much better.

How we think about ourselves and how we talk to ourselves on a daily is very important. When talking to yourself, stop, and think about how nice or mean you are talking. Think about it as if you were talking to your best friend. Some of the things we say to ourselves we would never say to a friend. We are our worst critics. Talking about ourselves is just as important. What we say to others is really what we think of ourselves.

Julie tells her co-workers the story of how she locked herself out of her apartment building a proceeded to say how stupid she was. Was she foolish, or did she just make a mistake? Give yourself a break; you are human. Think of yourself as your best friend and act accordingly.

Setting Goals and Achieving What You Want

It is essential to set goals. Goals help you keep going in the right direction. They actually give you direction. Tammy decided she wants to go to school and be a 4th-grade school teacher. She sets down and decides what needs to be done to achieve that goal. Then she takes little steps daily that will get her to this goal. She needs to get good grades in high school to get into the college she wants.   Each small goal will get her to the bigger ultimate goal.

Set goals and then set small goals. Small goals, you know you will achieve. This will give you small victories through the journey of the big one to keep you going. Sandy wants to lose 60 pounds in 6 months. This means she has to lose 2.5 pounds each week. She then puts in place a plan to eat right and exercise. The goals will not work unless you act upon the goal. Create a plan to put in place so that you will reach that goal. Each day needs to work towards that primary goal: big steps or little steps.

When Sandy reached a 30-pound weight loss, she celebrated by buying herself a new outfit to workout in. She had a manicure when she lost 40, and once the 60-pound weight loss goal was accomplished, she took herself to the beach for a week. Setting goals keeps you on track of the big picture. You may have to adjust what you are doing or how you do it from time to time but, staying consistent with the big goal is the main focus. Again, where your focus goes, your energy will flow - Tony Robbins.

Why is goal setting so important? It gives long term vision. If you have a goal, you will automatically create a plan to get yourself to that goal. It will teach you to stay organized and focused on what is important to you. Short term goals will help you stay focused, as well. They will be reached faster than in the long term. They will also help keep you motivated to succeed. Goals are a plan to get what you want out of life.

Ways to stick with it. Write your goals on post-it notes and plaster them everywhere, in the car, fridge, work, home office, bathroom mirror.

Be grateful for all that you have accomplished so far. Celebrate reaching your short-term goals when met. Keep a positive mental model of your goal. Think that you have completed your goal. Think about how you feel, what you will be wearing, and every detail you can think of. Hold that vision as long as you can each day.

Sara wants to be a famous country singer. She works hard and writes her own music and sings anywhere she can. Sara sees herself on stage with thousands of people watching her and singing her songs. Years go by, and finally, she gets a break to sing on stage for thousands of people. She's not nervous because for years she has envisioned this dream to be on stage. Now she just gets to enjoy the moment.

Set long term goals that may take years to achieve and set short term goals to help you stay motivated along the way. Create a plan and change the mental models that need to be changed in order to reach that goal. Keep going.

Tips to Change Your Mental Models to More Positive Thoughts

Be Grateful

I cannot stress this enough. If you are thinking about what you have and how far you have come in life how on earth can you be sad or feeling down? Now, pick something or someone you are grateful for and think about them or it daily. When you are feeling depressed or anxious about how far you still have to go in life, just stop, take a deep breath, and remember the thing or person that makes you happy.

Another great way to stay grateful is a gratitude journal. I am sure you can find the cute expensive ones on-line but, you can just take a journal or spiral notebook and write ten items you are grateful for each day. Some days you may only be thankful for a hot shower and your hot cup of coffee that morning. But, that's ok you will have that some days. Think about gratitude daily.

Create a Mantra

This one is helpful for focusing back on the positive mental models you have set in place. A mantra is somewhat of a prayer. It is a statement you tell yourself over and over when you feel overwhelmed or stress or just need a reminder that life will be ok. If you are struggling with money and all you think about is not having enough money to pay rent, then not having money will continue to flow your way. Remember where focus goes, energy flows.

Creating a mantra for not having enough money could be something like this. "I have abundance in all areas of my life." "Money flows easily and continuously to me." At first, you may not believe it but, keep saying it and start to believe it. Create the feeling of having money and what you would spend it on and how you would save it. Hold this feeling you have when you think about it. Focus on how you feel knowing you have money in the bank. This is how a mantra will help you develop a positive mental model.

Prove Yourself Wrong

The mind can lie to us. Tell us we can't possibly receive that promotion. I can't run a mini-marathon. You will never be able to find your soul mate. When these thoughts come to mind, and you know they are a lie but, you still believe them. Think about what you are thinking. Is it really true you can't run a mini-marathon? You may have already run several 5k races and maybe a ten miler. I think you can put in the training and run a mini-marathon. So, prove your mental model wrong. Set a goal and run a mini-marathon and create a new mental model that says you can run a mini-marathon because you did it.

Your energy will flow where your focus goes. Meaning if you think about the positive in your life, you will create more positive mental models and opportunities. Thinking that you can instead of you can't move you forward to the goal you have set for yourself. Knowing you can and will have or do something is a powerful tool to get what you want. Keep your focus positive in all areas of your life.

Get out of the Comfort Zone

Like I have said before this is a killer of dreams and motivation. When in the comfort zone, you choose to stay and not grow into the person you were meant to be. We all were meant for greatness in order to find that greatness we have to move outside of the comfort zone we have grown accustomed too. Do uncomfortable things and make us improve. Lisa wanted to run for class president but, she was so scared of failing, or no one voting for her she didn't run. The flip side of this would be she did run (getting out of her comfort zone) and won class president, and this started a successful career in politics. The most amazing things are on the other side of our comfort zone.

New Perspective

Taking a look at a situation from different angels could help in changing a mental model. Having a different look at a situation. Look at a positive way to think about it. See it from another person's view. View it as a positive instead of a negative.

Leah hates working overtime but, instead of complaining about it and being mad, she decided to look at it differently. She started to think about how much money she will earn working overtime. She decided that half of the money would go into saving which would put her over the goal she had set for herself for the month and the other half she would spend it on new clothes she needs for her trip next month.

In doing this, the time went by faster, and she was happy because her savings account was higher, and she would get to go shopping this weekend. Take a negative situation and create a positive out of it. Everything has a silver lining. Create mental models that support a positive outlook.

Improve the Moment

Becky was getting stressed at work. She had to finish this project before Friday. She was behind schedule and was overwhelmed with negative thoughts. After realizing she was overwhelmed and stressed, she stopped what she was doing, walked outside and took a deep breath. She sat in the sunlight and just thought about all she was grateful for. Thinking of her kids and how wonderful her life has been. Taking a moment and think about all the amazing people and things in your life will help you redirect your attention. Listen to music, dance, sing, do jumping jacks could also help you redirect. It will take your mind off of what is going on at the time and redirect your focus. After 15 minutes or so, Becky was ready to head back to work and get the project done. Less stressed and less overwhelmed than before.

There are thousands of ways to improve your mental models. Pick ones that will work for you. Listen to positive podcasts, meditate, journal, exercise. Do what feels good to you. Hobbies are a great way to redirect your mental models. The concentration that it takes on something you love creates a calmness in the brain. Create a plan to improve your mental models in a more positive way and watch your life change for the better.

Positive Thoughts

Be grateful and thank the Universe for the life you HAVE now. Desire more; it's your birthright to have all that you want. It's not selfish, and you aren't getting more than anyone else. The door is open for all of us to have all that we want, but we have to be willing to create the mental models and put in the work that it takes to get those things. Want to change your life financially, spiritually, and mentally?

Create new mental models that serve you, not hinder you. Make new positive mental models that will change your life for the better. The comfort zone will always hinder you. Live big. Remember what Tony Robbins always says, "Where focus flows energy will go."

Meaning what you put your focus on you will get more of. You keep telling yourself and others that you are broke and don't have a pot to piss in. Yep, that's what will stick around you and consume your life.

Turn it around and say and BELIEVE that your life is full of abundance in every way and notice when situations are going well and thank your Universe, God, Buddha. Gratitude is the number one thing that will put a positive spin on everything. How could you not be grateful when you are thinking about all that you hold dear in your heart? Your loved ones, kids, spouse, friends, the close parking space you got at the store. Every good thing is grateful.

The negative things are grateful. They are teaching you a lesson and help you create a better life. Keep positive mental models. Yes, you will have bad days, and that is human but, don't stay that way keep moving forward to be better. Create mental models on a morning routine that will help you set the tone for the day. Meditate, read, journal, exercise. Make time for yourself. I will repeat that. You have to MAKE time for yourself, or you will not take care of yourself. You will be busy taking care of everyone else.

Think of it this way. You can't pour water out of an empty cup, right? Fill your cup first so; you can fill everyone else's. You are not selfish for this. You are a better person, parent, friend, etc. Your cup is full; you can pour your love into others without feeling resentment. Filling your cup looks like a joy to you, whatever that means for you.

Taking a walk in nature, crafts, writing, being with loved ones, being by yourself. The thing that makes you happy do more of it. Be grateful for all that you have in your life. Once you start to have a new perspective on life, you will see your life begin to transform. It is just that easy. Easy to acknowledge sometimes hard to put in the work. Keep trying and keep changing life will become totally different.

Chapter 3: How Having A Team Mental Model Can Grow A Company

When a team or co-workers work together, it creates a spirit like no other. Everyone on the team feels heard, respected, and essential to the outcome of the project. Employees feel they can trust and depend on other co-workers to help them create and grow. A team learns the strengths and weaknesses of each team member. They support each other in all areas, strong or weak. An understanding and knowing that each member is supported by the others will grow a company to great success. When people or employees feel they are a part of something greater, they are willing to do more or "go the extra mile."

A company has to create a vision that the employees can believe in and want to help bring that vision to reality. Janet and Joel have a farm in which they raise grass-feed, no hormone beef cows. It is crucial for them to have the healthiest cows to pass along the healthiest beef to their customers. They are growing and needing to hire more employees. Finding others that share your same mental models about the company will help the company grow and will be easier to manage when the employees know what is expected of them and where the vision of the company is going. If the employees don't believe in the vision, then, problems will occur.

Problems will happen, but it will be solved together if the team is wanting the same vision. A vision gives the company direction and purpose. If the company vision is clear and sticks to the vision, then the company can survive for years to come. A company vision is a permanent goal that employees are striving for continuously.

Once the employees understand where the company wants to go, it is easier to work together towards that vision.

Janet and Joel want to keep their company growing but still, maintain the quality they always have had in the beef raising process. The employees will work alongside the owners to ensure that vision is upheld. They believe in the vision as much as the company or owners do.

Peter Senge is a pioneer in the way businesses are run today. He has created along with his colleagues a system called the learning organization system. This system creates teamwork and unity throughout a company. He had written a book on this system in 1990. The name of the book is "The Fifth Discipline." There are five pillars in the system to help a company succeed and be more productive. It will create unity within the company, and a closeness employee will cherish it.

The learning organization system is a system that lets the company as a whole grow along with the individuals. Learning and expanding enables a company to adapt to business needs and changes. The learning organization structure will keep the company ahead of the competition by providing new ideas and ways to do business. This will promote growth in the company. Employees learn, and so do the management team. It is a way to have everyone learning new fresh ideas to move the company forward. Learning can be exciting, and it will keep the employees on a more positive note as they use the new ideas they have learned and applying it to everyday work.

Build Sharing Vision

Build a sharing vision is the first of the five pillars. Build a shared vision can create excitement and togetherness throughout the company. The employees believe in the vision because they helped create the vision. When a learning organization system has established the company as a whole will be included, and everyone will get to share their ideas on the vision of the company. When all the employees of the company are all on the same page and very excited and can get behind the vision wholeheartedly then the employees will give more and do more because they feel as if they have a purpose and the vision is important to them just, as it is to the company. It creates an atmosphere of understanding and promotes kindness.

The shared vision is just what it says shared. Having that team player mental model will help everyone reach the same goal. It won't happen overnight, and it will take dedication from the management team and the employees but, a strong, understanding leader can help others feel the team spirit. The learning organization system will show employees that if a mistake is made, they will not be punished, but a conversation can occur to see what happened. The environment of this system will not have competition because everyone is helping one another.

Blaming others and ignoring the problem can corrupt everything a company is trying to accomplish. So, having an open, honest relationship with the employees will keep "peace" within the company. Let the employees know what the company is doing and why. Do not expect these changes to happen overnight. This is a process that the company will have to give it time to really take effect and change the inner workings of the company. If the company has a dedicated management team that cares about the employees and cleans up the office politics and helps the employees become better then, the company is on its way to becoming a learning organization business. The changes will create growth and expansion within the company.

Elizabeth attended a seminar about accounts receivables her company had sent her too. She had learned of a new software system that she thought would benefit her company. She was excited to discuss this new idea with co-workers and management. After everyone gave their input and concerns with the new system, they all agreed to give it a try. Elizabeth and her co-worker Tabetha would learn the system first and then teach everyone else.

By letting Elizabeth attend the seminar and then listening to what she thought about the idea and everyone discussing it.   The feeling that she mattered and everyone involved felt heard that made all the difference. This is why the learning organization system works so well. Everyone is treated equally, and everyone is heard.

System Thinking

System thinking is the second pillar. System thinking is the process of looking at a company as a whole and then looking at individual departments within the company to see how they affect each other. Each employee in each department will help the company strive to new heights by understanding its teamwork. Teamwork within the department and teamwork within the company. If working together, no matter how big or small the problem, if the employees work together, they will find the answers together.

When looking into system thinking, the best way to describe it is to look at an ecosystem. All the elements involved work together to survive together. The air, water, plants, animals, land everything. They all have a job, and in doing that job, they all survive together and become a "bigger picture." One does not work without the others, and if the balance of any has been compromised the system as a whole will suffer.

If the water becomes polluted, the fish will become ill, and the animals that eat the fish will become sick as well. The balance of the system has been interrupted.

The company as a whole depends on the individual employees that work for that company. If one department is failing, then the company is failing because that department needs help. Once the department gets the support, it needs then; all will be smooth again. Depending on each other in a company is what will help the company succeed. Understanding and compassion and continuous learning as employees and as a company will help the company grow.

In system thinking, the company also has to look to the past in order to see patterns or mistakes so they won't make them again. The company is always looking to improve, but, they also, have to be aware of their actions now that will negatively affect the company in the future. Google grew and was using massive amounts of energy. They started looking into renewable energy. Now, they are the world's largest renewable energy investor. Google was looking to the future, and they improved themselves and improved the planet. They were looking at the "big picture" and took advantage of it. Not, in a wrong way but, in a way that would help their vision and help the planet at the same time. Small pieces that fit together to make the big picture. This is how system thinking works.

Mental Models

Mental models are a massive part of the success or failure of a company. The mental models are the way the company as a whole, thinks. They are also how employees think. The company's vision is a mental model. It is how the company sees itself in the world. The employees also know the vision of the company and how they fit into the vision. How can they create value for that vision? The vision of a company stays, the same, but, the mental models can change and still honor the vision.

The company is clear on the vision. To feed school kids in their school district healthy, satisfying meals for lunch. Different mental models will have different ways of doing this. Using the ideas of the employees to solve the problem of how they will make this happen. This will create teamwork and will help the team trust and respect each other because everyone is being heard.

Mental models are the way we look at the world. We all look at the same problem differently because we all have different backgrounds. We all have different childhoods, experiences, beliefs, ideas. The list goes on and on.

With different mental models, it can create one solution to solve the problem at hand.

Mental models for business can change, and the company has to be willing to be flexible and adapt to the changes that need to be made to move forward and become a company that will last. Growing and learning will improve mental models. Learning new ways to think will create new connections and new mental models that will serve the individual and the company. The company has to be willing to make mental model changes often to keep up with the changing world of business.

Sales are down in a company. The company looks at the data and decides to have a meeting with the sales team. The company is not judging or criticizing the sales team; they are just interested in why the sales are down. The employees express how the current sales pitch isn't working the same as it once has.

Lisa, one of the salespeople, invites the idea of changing the way they are doing it. After, much discussion, the sales team, and the company come together and starts to create a new plan on how to approach new customers. With all the sales teams working together they come up with a great ideal that works both for the sales team and the company. The next month sales are doubled. The sales team shifted mental models and created a new one that felt good to use.

Team Learning

Team learning is the concept of coming together and solving a problem together. Through discussion, brainstorming, and collaboration, team learning will show your employees how to work out problems together, as a group.

Team learning can foster creativity and learning. When people are put together to reach a common goal, creativity cannot help but, show up. The ideas of everyone coming together will spark excitement and create a different perspective on the situation at hand. The viewpoints of each person will be different, and this will help create a solution that will work for everyone. The unique perspective from each individual in the group wlll bring new light to the problem. When working with a team, the team has each other to bounce ideas off of. Even if the idea isn't a great one, it still may spark a better one from someone else. It gives shy employees a chance to be heard and will provide them with the confidence to speak up.

It also creates enthusiasm within the group because ideas are being shared, and discoveries are being made. Learning is vital, but learning in a group promotes teamwork, creativity, and builds trust among employees.

Mr. Short teaches 4th-grade math. He divided the students up into four groups. Gave each group a different problem to solve. The groups of kids or teams had to work together to figure out the answer, and they couldn't cheat by asking another group the answer. The students had to rely on each other to figure out the solution. By putting their knowledge and understanding of the problem together, they could come up with the correct answer. They would have to work together in order to create the right solution. One common goal but different ideas on how to get the answer.

Personal Mastery

Personal mastery is the practice of improving oneself. In order for a person to understand oneself, they have to be willing to explore and look within to find the true self. Not the self, everyone else wants them to be but, who they really are deep down inside. Personal development is a perfect way to start to understand the mental models you have about yourself. How some mental models are not serving you and knowing you can change them? Personal development doesn't mean you are broken and need to be fixed. Personal development is a tool to help you understand yourself better.

A way to improve yourself in order to get the life you want. Personal development can be mediation, books, podcasts, classes, yoga, anything that will enhance your life in a fulfilling way. Creating the life, you want takes time and lessons have to be learned. Focus and intent will help you through. Personal mastery means different things to different people, and there are many ways to reach this level. Take responsibility for your victories and failures. You make the choices, and you have to deal with the consequences of those choices.

Changing the beliefs and mental models you have of yourself and learning to construct ones that will serve you better is a big step in becoming the person you want to be. Not everyone will like the changes you will be making to get to the goals you have set for yourself. Learning to deal with others and still be true to yourself is a challenge at times. But, understand the changes in yourself will make you proud. You will continue to learn to "up your game" to continue to be the person you have always wanted to be. Personal mastery is the ability to be comfortable with who you are. Where you are in your life and still strive to be better and love yourself more.

Selfcare plays a big part in personal mastery. You have to take care of yourself FIRST. I repeat taking care of yourself FIRST will help you take care of others.

Carrie is a stay at home mom of 3. Ages six, three, and a year old. She takes care of the children all day. Doing for them all that needs to be done. Feeding, cuddling, changing diapers, wiping runny noses, and the list goes on and on.

By the end of the day, she is spent. She is so tired and easily irritated, that she breaks down and starts to cry because the six-year-old wouldn't stop asking her questions about why dogs poop. This mother is not taking care of herself.

Selfcare is non-existing. How could she handle the situation differently? By taking time for herself. While the kids are napping, she could be reading a book, meditating, taking a nap with them, listening to a podcast while she cleans the house. Anything that will improve herself and fill her cup. There is an old saying, "You can't pour from an empty cup." Meaning if you don't have anything left to give, you will not be able to give to others. Doing things that bring you joy and happiness and make you feel at peace. Those are the things you need to do more of and more often. Remember it is your life, live it the way YOU want to live it. You will be happy if you do.

Creating a Vision for the Company That Everyone Will Get Behind

When creating a vision personal or business, the vision has to touch your soul. It has to mean so much to you that you are willing to do the work necessary to see it come to life. In business, the vision has to be one to better the world. That's why businesses exist right? To provide service or product to make life easier and better. Yes, some businesses are not going about it in the correct moral way. Most businesses want to make the world a better place.

In creating a vision, it should be something employees can believe in and WANT to bring the vision to reality with the company. A vision for a company should convey where a company wants to be and how they want to help their customers be there with them in a better place. Understanding where the customer wants to be and explaining how the company can get them there makes the customer "feel" like they are a part of something bigger or apart of the family. In creating a vision for the company, the customer should be the number one reason.

When employees believe they can move mountains with a company's vision, they are more willing to work towards making that vision come true day in and day out. If the company vision is to create shoes that will make your feet feel happy and also, help starving children in Africa with every pair sold. That is a powerful vision that people want to be a part of. They will be committed themselves along with the company to provide all that they are stating. The power of a company vision is fantastic.

If the company allows the employees to have an input with the company vision, they will feel a part of the "big picture." They feel they have a voice and that the company cares about what the employees have to say and the ideas they have. They feel heard and feel important. That is all that humans want. They want a voice, and they want to feel they matter. Create a vision with the employees, and the company will have a trust that will help them grow and expand into greater things. As long as the vision stays true to the company and the employees are involved in some way. The company is more likely to have success and last for years to come.

A small company asked employees to submit an idea for the company vision. When all the ideas were collected, the company held a meeting and read the opinions and let the employees pick their favorite one, and the vision was born. The employees felt pride and a feeling of family because they were involved. Bring the team/employees together, and creativity will flow freely.

Creating Space for Employees to Grow Will Improve Business

We all want to improve ourselves in some way or another. We have a deep-rooted desire to be fulfilled. We need connection and love with other humans. At some point in life, we discover something is missing, or we have a longing for more or different. We get a glimpse of what our life might be like. We hear instructions to do things that are totally out of the norm for us. If we listen, we will discover that whisper is just what we need. Our soul aches to be heard. Some may think of this as silly and a total crock. Others believe and understand the importance of taking care of yourself and listening to that voice.

You own a profitable coffee shop. You have considered hiring someone for marketing and social media accounts. One day you are sitting in the back working on paperwork. A voice tells you to go out front to help serve tables. So, you listen to the voice and go out front to help with the afternoon crowd.

The first table you come to is two women, the first woman is discussing marketing and social media accounts and telling the other one how she could free up her time by letting her run them for her. She was just what you need. You ask for her card and make plans to discuss your own needs. The Universe, God, Buddha, was helping you get what you needed.

How is all of this important to business? If the employees are happy, they are more productive. This sounds shallow and selfish for the company to state, but, it's true. If a company can offer tools to improve the employee's life both personally and professionally, that company cares about its employees. Having information available and continuous open communication about what the employees want, and need will help the employees balance life.

The company can offer yoga classes or give a discount to the local gym. Offer discounts on meditation retreats. Have classes to promote self-care and encourage spirituality by inviting inspirational speakers to speak and motivate healthy, positive mental models. Helping the employees learn to take care of themselves as a whole will help them deal with the pressures and demands at work and in personal life. The more a person takes care of themselves, the more balanced in life they are. Again, happy employees are productive employees.

Understand I am not saying this will be rainbows and unicorns all the time. It takes time for a person to discover they want something more for their life. Not all employees will be willing to change quickly. It may take a while, but having the tools they need to improve will make the transition easier.

Rita knew she wanted more for her life but wasn't sure what to do or where to start. At work, she had seen the company was offering free tickets to a motivational speaker. Rita thought this would be a great place to start. After attending the seminar, she heard a little voice telling her to go back to school. Rita had always wanted to be a nurse. Now, she is a nurse at the company that gave her the tickets, to see the speaker, that changed her life. Be that company. The company that offers tools for the employees to better themselves and help balance their lives. This balance of life will also include work life. A happy employee is a productive employee.

Becoming a Better Leader and What It Will Take

To succeed in any business, the company needs strong leadership. This leadership has the ability to create a workspace that will help the employees as well, as the company. There are certain factors that go into a good leader. The leaders of a company have a clear vision of the company in order to relay that to the employees. The mental models and attitude that a leader has will trickle down to the employees that work under them.

If the leader is positive and enthusiastic about what needs to be done daily, even if it isn't her favorite thing to do, the employees will learn this attitude and mental model from him. He leads by example. When the employees see Hendrix following the rules and implementing what the company has put into place, they are more apt to follow. The leaders shouldn't be held to a different standard as the employee. If a mistake is made, they should be held accountable for the error just as the employees are.

Communication is one of the critical tools a leader can have. This way, the employees know what he expects out of them, and he knows what the employees expect of him. Open communication will bring trust into the company byways of letting everyone be heard. The company will feel more as a team if everyone is able to voice ideas and concerns without being punished or disregarded. Even if the idea wasn't implemented, the employee still felt heard.

When conflict or difficult conversations come up, the leader has to be able to convey what needs to transpire. Communication isn't only for resolving disagreements or conflicts; it is also, great for relaying ideas and how we can problem-solve together. If employees and management are talking and understanding what is expected of each of them, then, the company as a whole will be stronger. Everyone is understanding clearly what is expected. Using simple manners will go a long way, as well. Please and thank you hold respect for the individuals. Showing appreciation lets a person know they make a difference. That will go a long way in a company.

The leader should have compassion and empathy for the employees and understand what they are going through and how they feel. The leader should know his people. Know them on a personal level. If Jamie's mother has breast cancer, then, the leader should know this and consider asking how her mother is doing and how Jamie is doing. If Walter is going through a divorce and his work is suffering, a leader would ask what is going on instead of just assuming Walter is lazy and slacking.

People want to know others' care, and a great leader will relay that to their people. For a leader to have emotional intelligence skills will help the leader resolve conflict and promote team mental models. Understand how the employees feel, and the concerns they have will help the leader be better equipped to resolve conflict and disagreements. Choosing their words will also help a leader dissolve a disagreement. The leader should have compassion and empathy for the employees. Understanding the employees will give you an advantage on how to deal with problems that arise.

A good leader with team-building skills will promote the idea that everyone's opinion count and the views and concerns will be heard. Not everyone's plan may be used, but everyone voiced their idea. Keeping employees or team motivated is essential. Daily routines can take a toll on the team to stay motivated. This is where a leader can encourage and create challenges to improve motivation. Tish noticed that her employees were losing motivation as the month went on. A lot of projects needed to be finished and the company was under a lot of pressure to complete several big ones. Tish noticed this lack of motivation and gathered everyone together and took them outside for a break in the sun. They threw a football, and others just sat and enjoyed the sun. Once back inside the team seemed to be more focused and back on track.

The leader needs to notice how the team is functioning and what the needs of the team are. Being clear on their needs will help operations move more smoothly, and the employees will be willing to be loyal to the company. The company takes care of the employees; the employees will take care of the company. This will also create trust between management and employees. It will be earned over time, but it will be created.

Employees will trust a company more when the company does what they say they will. If a company announces a 500 dollar bonus at the end of the month because sales are up and then, when the end of the month comes, they don't follow through with that promise. Not only will the employees be mad, but the employees also will not trust what a company says, and that will start the dismantling of that company. The company has to do what they say they will do. They ask that of the employees, the company should be responsible for doing that as well.

The leader of a company will also understand the importance of team-building skills in different situations. Of course, conflict and disagreements but, just keeping the team or company in alignment with the vision of the company. Help the employees stay on task and focus on the crucial issues. A well-rounded leader will have all of the skills. They may be stronger in one area more than others but, having the knowledge and ability to want to help make a company and employees better is a sign of success for a company. The leader should be able to empathize and have the emotional intelligence to resolve and improve the situations that come up.

Leading by example will also, instill that rules also, apply to leaders as well as employees. A leader that shows they care about their team will know each person on a personal level. If the performance of an employee changes for the worse or even better, a good leader will notice this and ask questions to find out why performance is suffering or give them encouragement for a job well done. The leader has to be willing to support the employees the best way he knows how. Keeping lines of communications open and both knowing what is expected of them will help build the trust a company needs to grow and expand.

A leader needs to be fair and honest. Helping resolve problems among employees by teaching them how to do it themselves. Assisting with the problem, not resolving it for them. Teaching them this will encourage team-building skills and open communication between employees.

Positive Thoughts

Let the employees know you care. The leader has to show that they care on a personal level. The leader understands what is going on in the private lives of their employees. Personal life affects work life. They are helping employees be a team player and build skills that will help them throughout their work-life careers. Know when the team needs a break, or a little encouragement will help keep the team motivated and not be burned out on the daily routine.

The company has to understand that their employees are people, not robots. Take care of the employees, and they will take care of the company. Understand the needs and let the employees express their ideas and concerns. Let them be heard even if their ideas aren't used. The simple act of acknowledging them will keep them loyal and happy. The company has to be true and clear on the vision they have. When the company knows where they want to be, it is easier to let the employees know as well. The employees will have a clear path of what they need to do to get the company to that vision.

A good leader will have empathy and compassion for the employees. The leader will understand what the employees need. This will instill support and trust between the leader and the employees. When a leader gives to the employees, the employees will give back. If the leader is giving gratitude and support the employees will respond by giving the same back. The jobs they do on a daily will reflect the respect they have for their leader. A genuine caring attitude will take a team a lot farthing then, an attitude of resentment and lack of respect.

So, just be a good person and listen to the employees. They will tell you what needs to be addressed and what is working. Trust them, and they will trust the company.

Chapter 4: Different Areas of Mental Models and How They Can Be Changed

There are several areas that mental models are created and can be changed. In this chapter, we will explore the different areas and start to understand how we develop mental models and why. Changing mental models is a process and will take time. Some models will be easy to change, and some will not. Understanding how they work for us or against us is essential. If we are aware of the mental models, we can change them. Improving these areas will enhance your life and give you new insight into changing the mental models you need to change in order to provide you with the amazing life you want.

The brain is a fantastic tool to get what we want and to understand the world we live in. Create mental models that serve you. Knowledge is the power to move forward. Trust that you can create what you want for yourself. Whatever that looks like for you. Tools to sharpen your mind now can help you ward off Alzheimer's later in life as well as living your best life now.

There are different things you can do to improve your memory and thinking process. Eating a healthy diet and drinking plenty of water fuels the brain and helps it function properly. Getting enough exercise will help you release stress and "clear your mind." Helpful chemicals in the brain will be released, and new connections will be made. Meditation has been proven to quiet the mind and bring peace and balance to the person that is using it. The list for improving your brain and your health are endless. Find something that works for you and continue to do it. If after time that doesn't seem to work for you anymore, then decide to try something new. It is not set in stone what is the right or wrong way to bring peace to your mind.

Memory and How It Works

There are different areas of memory. The long-term memory will store, retrieve, and organize memories. Short-term memory is information that hasn't been decided to dismiss or store into long-term memory. Explicit memory is a long-term memory that you will have to concentrate on remembering them. Recalling a certain memory. Implicit memory is remembering from repetitiveness, subconscious "auto-pilot." Autobiographical memory is a memory you can recall more vividly than others.

Long-Term Memory

For memories to become long-term memories, it will have to impact you in some way. Big or small, you will remember it for years to come. You can recall it and may remember all of it or just a few sections of it. These are what we base our future upon. These memories are gathered and organized, so when a situation comes up again; we will be more prepared for it. The thought of getting on a roller coast may make you instantly recall a memory of you getting sick on a roller coaster when you were twelve. The mind will remind you not to get on the roller coaster because last time you felt ill. Long-term memory will store everything that happens to us.

If we didn't have long-term memory, we would not be able to continue to have relationships or have a conversation. The long-term memory is what retains all the information that allows us to do these things. The schooling we have had and everything that we have learned from our parents or teachers. Thinking about the things you do on a daily couldn't be done without long-term memory. It is the life behind all that we do. The long-term memory is critical to maintaining the life we have created.

Short-Term Memory

The mind takes in so much information on a second by second bases. Some of the information we need and some we don't. Short-term memory is where we take in all of this information. Our brain decides if we need to dismiss it or if we need to store it into long-term memory. Working the memory muscle will help you strengthen your mind now and help ward off Alzheimer's later in life. Studies have shown that practicing brain games will increase new connections and boost your brain to stay healthy.

Short-term memory is how the waiter at your favorite restaurant takes your order and doesn't write it down. They are exercising their memory muscles. The short-term memory can only hold a limited amount of information for about 20 to 30 seconds. That is why repeating the information will help you retain it better. When you first met someone, Hi Connie. I am glad to meet you, Connie. Doing this will help you remember the person's name.

Explicit Memory

Explicit memory is recalling a memory and intentionally remembering the memory. You try to remember vivid details when you think hard enough about the memory. This is the memory you have when you smell apple pie, and you think of your grandmother's house at Thanksgiving time. There are two different types of explicit memory. One is episodic, which is your memory of your name, childhood, and family relationships. The other is semantic memory which is random knowledge like the capital of Kentucky is Frankfort. When remembering a memory if two or more senses are recalled, the memory will be easier to recall.

Implicit Memory

Implicit memory is a memory that we don't have to think about it. The subconscious memory takes over. The repetition of this task just happens. We don't have to think about it. It is the route we take home. We know this route so well we sometimes forget if we stopped at the stop sign before entering the neighborhood. Assembly line workers use implicit memory daily. Missing parts or a defect will send a red flag in the brain, letting the worker know it isn't right because it will look different from the last 300 parts, they have seen that day. The subconscious mind will take over and let the conscious mind think of other things.

Autobiographical Memory

This memory you can recall better than other memories. Autobiographical memory falls in with explicit memory, but what makes it different is you can remember it and feel like you are there right back where you were in the memory. Autobiographical memory is highlighted with more than one sense. Trent remembers working on his grandfather's farm when he smells wet hay and sees a field of horses. Vividly remembering is autobiographical memory.

Critical Thinking

Critical thinking is looking at an issue or situation with the facts and coming up with a conclusion or solution. There are five skills we use when talking about critical thinking. The first is analytical. Analytical is when we ask questions to find out more information to create a decision. We use data and facts about the situation or event to determine how we see the world. A person will ask questions to find more information in order to help make a decision. Communication is essential to relay your idea or answer to others in a way that they can understand and understand your point of view. It will help get information and give information to make the decision for the situation.   If your conclusions are relayed clearly, others can understand what is being said, and that can help them make their own decisions.

Creativity is a way of looking at a problem and finding a new way to solve it. Creativity promotes curiosity, imagination, and new thinking. When critical thinking uses an open-mind, it is able to set aside emotions, assumptions, and judgments. A decision is made based on facts and data. The decision or solution will be fair and unbiased.

Problem-solving contracts the facts and data that the analytical brain has gathered and organizes that information to understand the problem, based on that information, the brain can start to solve the problem. Decide on the best way to handle the situation. Problem-solving will make clarifications and have a conclusion.

Analytical Thinking

In this stage of the problem-solving dilemma, the brain gathers the information that will later give us the tools to create a resolution to the problem at hand. It is always seeking information. The information coming into the brain starts to be organized and shuffled to make sense of what the outside world is doing. At this stage, mostly what is happing is just getting the information, assessing the situation, and looking for an answer to the problem.

Analytical thinking uses the sense to gather information. A person has been transported to a hospital after a severe car accident. The emergency room nurse will start to evaluate the person and ask questions to gather information to help improve the patient's health and current situation. Watching vitals and how the patient is responding to different evaluations will determine how the nurse will take the steps needed to save this patient's life. Analytical thinking gathers the information in the world so the brain can determine the solution to the current problem.

A great way to create a stronger analytical thinking skill is to practice. Walkout in the world and just observe the surroundings. Be aware of what is going on, look at details, and notice what you are interested in. Create questions about how things work and understand the concept. Games are another great way to improve the analytical mind. Research online and find brain games that will help you improve your brain function. When resolving a problem, look at the pros and cons of the issue. Be intentional in your decision making and recognize the consequences of your decision.

Communication Skill

This is important in all aspects of your life. In relationships and in problem-solving. If you have discovered a link or resolution to a problem and need to relay the information to someone else, your communication skills should be clear and direct. The tone we use to say it will also, help understand the information. If you are able to share information effectively and use terminology that your audience can understand it will be a benefit to you and the audience. Having excellent communication skills with verbal as well as written will help you relay critical information.

Jason has a great idea to change the kitchen so that it will flow and be more efficient. In relaying this idea to his wife, he has to be clear on where the table, appliances, cabinets will be placed. Jason created a diagram that showed where everything will be set and what walls need to be taken out or moved. Having clear information, you and the person can have a better understanding of the problem.

A great way to improve communication skills is to talk to different people with different views. Get new perspectives on the issues that mean the most to you.

Find yourself a pen pal and start to write or email friends and explain the ideas that you have. Make communication a priority each day. Learning a new word a day and use it throughout the day. Check on the internet for games that will enhance your communication skills.

Creativity Skills

Creativity is in every one; there are lots of ways to express it. Some people are creative in an artistic way like most people think about painting, sculpture, drawings. But there are other ways to be creative. Being creative is looking at the world in a different way than what you usually see it. Creativity skills are fueled by imagination and curiosity. Creative thinking may also be called "thinking outside the box." This way of thinking will help create solutions to daily human problems. Asking questions of why something is working or not will help start your creative thinking.

Trying to create something new daily or even weekly will boost your creativity. When we learn something new, it opens pathways in our brain to make new connections; these connections can help you have a unique perspective on situations that will change your life for the better. Each day Justin draws a picture of something a chair, cat, friend. Some days it will be a doodling or other days more elaborate and detailed drawing, but each day he will draw something.

Being devoted instead of disciplined will help you feel "freer" with the situation instead of making it a chore and feel controlled. Learning to change your mental models to perceive life in a different way could help make it a pleasant experience instead of a dreaded one.

Creating can be fun, and having a good time doing it will stimulate the area of your brain that likes the reward system. Tiffany is learning to play the drums; each day, she will play a different part of a song until she gets it right. The devotion she has and the desire to play the drums makes it fun but, discipline and demand would make it seem more like a chore to her.

Open-Mindedness

Having an open-mind for solving problems can be challenging at times. Keeping an open mind means you have to take the emotions, judgment, and assumptions out of the decision-making process. We are human, and all of these issues come naturally to us, so taking them out of the equation can be challenging at times. Open-minded people are more accepting of others and seem to be more optimistic. Open-minded people see issues and situations from both sides. They learn from others and adapt to enjoying life more. Easily adaptable to change because they are willing to see things differently.

Samantha and Allen are discussing what color to paint the living room. Allen was set on painting it bright blue. Samantha wanted a lighter shade to brighten up the room because it didn't have a lot of natural light. After explaining to Allen that the dark blue would make the room seem smaller and more cluttered, he realized that the lighter color would be a better option. He looked at both sides of the conversation and saw Samantha's idea on the room color made more sense. Looking at a problem from everyone's perspective will open more significant discussions and may even change people's attitudes to a more open-minded way.

Consider seeing both sides of an issue or even an argument. Having a firm grip on how the other person sees the problems or situations will give you a better overall view of how to resolve the issue. You don't have to believe what the other person believes but, trying to understand where they are coming from will help solve any problems that may occur.

Practice the urge to control emotional response to the point of view you don't agree with. Listen to what the person has to say and have them explain anything that isn't clear. Ask questions if you don't understand but, try and keep your emotions out of the conversation. Listen to the facts and try to understand what is being said; it doesn't mean you have to be convinced of their view, but it will help you understand where they are coming from.

Problem-Solving

Problem-solving is about generating and implementing a solution to a problem. Finding the facts and figuring out a way to resolve the problem will take the other skills to help resolve the issues. Problem-solving is the plan to create a solution. Step by step, organizing facts to lead to the final resolution to the situation.

Using the other skills to help create a plan to conclude the problem is beneficial in determining how the problem will be fixed.

Jacob is having trouble solving the mathematical problem in class today. He took the math problem home and asked his mother if she could help him understand how to solve it. She explained the problem to him, and after clarification, he created a plan to solve the problem. Checking the facts and understanding a systematical way of creating an outline is how problems are resolved.

Great ways to improve your problem-solving skills is by using language that promotes ideas. "What if" or "Imagine if" were the questions you were asking yourself to create a solution. Anything is possible; you just have to create a way to spark your thought process.

Focus on the solution, not the problem. When you are thinking in terms of a solution, the problem isn't the focus the solution is. So, in turn, where focus goes is where energy will flow.

Look for obvious answers. Keep it simple and return to the basics. Humans tend to overthink issues and situations, and it only complicates finding a solution. Start by looking at it in the simplest way, sometimes that will give us the answer we have been looking for.

Another tool to help discover the answer to a problem is asking yourself the right questions. The five why's will help you figure out the root cause of the problem.

Josie is late to work.

Why is she late to work? She was tried and hit the snooze button.

Why was she tired? Stayed up to late the night before.

Why did she stay up too late? She took a nap after work yesterday.

Why did she take a nap after work? She was watching her nephew.

Why was she tired of watching her nephew? They played a lot.

Asking yourself the simple question "why" will bring you back to the root cause of the problem. If you know the reason, you can start to fix the problem.

Starting to solve a problem takes several different aspects of looking at the problem. We have to gather data and the facts (analytical) and determine what the best solution to the problem would be by looking at all perspectives. (open-minded) And then discover how we will relay this information to others to get the plan in action to start solving the issue (communication). Using a new way to look at the problem will teach you how to "think outside the box," these ideas can come from others or within you. (creativity).

Decision-Making

Decision-making is finding the best solution for a situation or issue by using beliefs, facts, values that align with you. It reflects what beliefs, perspectives, values, and how emotionally involved you are with the situation. The above factors all play a part in the final decision.

Decision-making and problem-solving are not the same, as problem-solving facts and data are the main elements with no emotions or judgment. Decision-making emotions are part of the decision.

Jason was offered a new position across the country, doing a different job completely. His emotions will play a part in the decision because he will be leaving his home town to pursue this job. It can be scary to leave everything you have known. Decision-making is more personal and tailored to you. It will ultimately be your decision. The decision that is made isn't right or wrong; it is what best fits your needs or wants.

Rational Decision Making

Rational decision making is how the majority of the population creates a solution. Weighing the options and viewing the pros and cons to decide on the correct decision for them. This decision-making style uses the facts and information and logical thinking to create a solution that will be the right answer based on the facts that have been given. Rational decision making will consider consequences; if I make this decision, then this will happen, and so on.

Joe has two job offers; one is in Hawaii, and the other is in Canada. Joe has wanted to live in both places; both companies are similar. His decision will be based on facts and what each company has to offer. Deciding the pros and cons of each company and place will help Joe make a clear decision on what job to take.

When making a rational decision, the first thing you will have to do is define the problem. In Joe's case, it was where to live and what company to choose. After the problem is determined, the next step will be to ask yourself a series of questions that will promote the outcome of the decision. Looking at the choices and how it will affect others is the third part of rational thinking.

Including others that will be affected by this decision is part of the process that may make it a little harder. The fourth step is to create an alternative list. A list you may not use but, other options that you could consider. Doing this will lead to alternative results and thinking ahead to see how each decision will end and weighing the options.

Leo owns a catering company, and he needs to hire another employee but, isn't sure where to create the money for one. He starts to ask himself where he is wasting money or could save money. When and if he does hirer another person how much more money would that bring in because he could add more events to his calendar. Leo creates a list of all the pros and cons of hiring another person. Would he make more money even if he is paying another person to help? Considering the income could be beneficial as well. Leo looks at the data and facts on hiring a new person, and now he can decide what will work best for him. Weighing the options and getting a clear understanding of the information and facts will help make the right decision for the situation.

Consider the facts and try to keep your emotions out of the decision if you want to make a clear conscious decision that will serve you.

Make a list of the pros and cons of the situations. Listings the good points and the bad points will be helpful in creating a rational decision. Consider all the alternatives and the consequences and how it will affect others along with yourself and then pick the best one.

Intuitive Decision Making

Intuitive decision making is more of a decision based on how you "feel." It is a knowing inside yourself, and you have no doubt about the situation or issue and what you should do. There isn't a doubt you are making the right decision. The facts and data and rational thinking doesn't make a difference in this process or even help. Sometimes it's a voice that will tell you that it is the right decision or it is a feeling in your body like butterflies in your stomach when you think about the choice you need to make. Facts and data will not help make the decision; it is based on a "gut" feeling.

Intuitive decisions are made quickly, not a lot of thought goes into making these decisions. The situation presents itself, and you respond by the way your body feels or the voice that speaks to you at that moment. It feels right to you, so you go with the flow of how you feel. It is hard to explain because the facts are not a part of the equation, and you don't rely on the data and facts. There is nothing to tell you if it is right or wrong, you just "feel" that it is the right thing to do for you at the time. You can't explain this feeling that comes over you. It is just in your knowing.

Ericka knew that she would find true love, but she wasn't sure when it would happen. A co-worker set her up on a blind date. Ericka was hesitant to go, but she heard a voice that told her to go out with this guy. After spending 10 minutes with Todd, she was convinced that he was her soul mate. They couldn't explain it, but they just knew they were meant to be together. Six months later, they were married. They both felt the certainty and Ericka heard her inner voice telling her Todd was the one for her.

A person can increase the listening factor to their intuition. When you listen to the intuition more often and realize what is going on, you are in tune with it. You understand what is going on and are willing to listen to it. It will take time to know when your inner self is talking but, the more you listen and practice, the better you will know when it is talking to you. Remember the feelings you had gotten when it had happened before, and you realized what was going on.

Sometimes it is a tightness in your stomach; other times, it is hair standing up on the back of your neck. You will begin to learn what the signs are for you. Be sure to pay attention to your first impulse, that initial feeling, voice, knowing will be the answer that you are looking for. Yes, some decisions you should research if you are unsure, but when you are asked a question, and you blurt out an answer and then wonder where that came from that is your intuition talking. The intuition will not lead you down the wrong road; it will always put you where you need to be at the time even if that doesn't align with where you think you should be. The inner knowing will always put, you in the right place and time for what you need to have at the time.

Practice and listening to the feedback will help you tune into your inner knowing. Kate was sitting at a stoplight when the light turned green, she felt a tug in her heart to wait before she took off, so she did. Two seconds later, another car was running a red light going way to fast. He would have hit her if she took off. Remember how it feels when you get that feeling in your body. Remember when you were a teenager, and you went to the party but, the whole time you had a sick feeling that you shouldn't? You didn't listen to the sign, and two hours later the cops show up and break up the party. That feeling everyone has experienced at some point or another in their life.

Knowing you shouldn't do something and you do it anyway and the end result turns out horrible. The feeling you should do something but, you don't, and you miss a golden opportunity to meet your favorite band. Start to listen and start to notice the feelings or voice more. Be aware of how you feel; remember that feeling. Start obeying that knowing. You will be surprised how your life will change, and you will start to have more happiness in your life.

Positive Thoughts

Start to believe and trust yourself. You know what is best for your life and no one else knows better than you. You could base your decision off your "gut" feeling and just let the inner knowing guide you or you could be a more rational thinker and weigh your options and make pro and con lists, collect the data, determine the outcome of the decision. There isn't a wrong way to do this, it is your life, and you know what is best for you. The choice for your life is your decision; it can't be wrong.

Overthinking is common on big decisions; at times, you need to take it back to the basics and keep it simple.

Believe in yourself and trust the inner self to guide you in the right direction even if you have no idea where that voice is taking you. You will be successful, and you will know in your heart what is right for you. Listen to it and do what it says even if you think it is crazy what it is telling you. Make sure you are listening to the little things, so when it is time to make the big decisions, you will know exactly how you are to feel.

Make your lists and collect your data and facts. Doing this will help you make the decision clear but don't forget to consider others that will be affected by this decision. Doing your homework will make a difference if it is right for you or not. Combining rational and intuitive decision making can almost guarantee that it is the right decision for you. Listening to your inner voice, intuition, "gut" or whatever you want to call, it will help you be more in tune with your intuition to help you make better decisions for your life.

Chapter 5: Being Aware of Your Mental Models Is the First Step to Changing

Negative mental models are playing in our minds daily, and most of the time, we don't even realize it is happening or if we do realize, we just keep doing it. It is a constant loop of negative thoughts that is on autoplay. Some of us have had negative talk going on so long; we just think it is the norm. When you spill coffee on the counter, we mumble "stupid" or "you're so clumsy." When a mistake at work is made, we start to bombard ourselves with mean thoughts that we would never consider saying to our kids or best friend. If others speak ill of themselves, we are quick to correct them but, we don't take our own advice. We are our own worst critic.

To define what is meant by a negative thought or mental models in this context is the mean, unpleasant, degrading dialogue we have about ourselves in our own mind.

How do we stop or redirect our negative thinking? The first step is to start to be aware of the things you are saying and when you are saying them. Tamara was using the copier, and there was a paper jam. It wasn't her fault; she was just using it. She starts to say things like "I cannot believe you did this!" "Why do they let you use the copier?" For one, it isn't her fault; the copier has been getting jammed for weeks. Is all that negative talk really necessary? Tamara may just start to say these things and not even realize she is doing it. That is how powerful the mind is. We believe what it tells us even if it isn't true. The mental models we have created just kick in and tell us what we have been telling ourselves for years.

At times we forget that we have a choice about what we say and do. Once you notice the negative talk has started, you can listen to it and see what it is saying, or you could stop, take a breath, and then decide a more positive thing to say to yourself. Listening to the negative talk will help you realize you are actually telling the mean things to yourself. Listening will also help you understand where the mental model came from. Maybe the voice you hear is your mother's or what you are saying was something your father told you all the time. These are great ways to find the root cause of these mental models. When you know where they came from or when they started, that can help unravel the old mental model and create new ones that will serve you better.

Kristen started college, and she had noticed when she didn't do well on a test, the negative dialogue would start. The thoughts of not being smart enough, good enough, or worthy of receiving a degree in science would start. She would feel depressed and anxious. The more she thought about this negative mental model, the more she began to understand where it had started.

She had put the pressure on herself because she thought her dad would be disappointed in her for not doing well on the test. This led to her thinking he didn't love her. She traced this back to the fifth grade when she failed a math quiz, and she knew her dad would be upset. He wasn't but, she kept believing he was. In turn, this started the process of not being good enough when she didn't pass a test in school.

The mind is a powerful tool that can be used for us or against us. It is up to us to take control back and decide to create a better life for ourselves.

Science has proven we are on autopilot 85 to 95 percent of the time. Autopilot means that we are not consciously thinking about what we are doing. Autopilot is when you come home from work, and you ask yourself if you stopped at the stop sign at the end of the street. You do it so much your brain doesn't really THINK about doing it. Anything you do the same day in and day out may be considered autopilot. If we send this much time in our subconscious maybe it would be a good idea to listen to what it is telling us on a daily? The subconscious remembers everything, the times your parents yelled at you for misbehaving when you were six and the time your father was disappointed in you when you were seventeen.

These stories stick with us and create mental models that tell us we are not worthy or that we aren't smart enough to be in college. We continue to believe the negative mental models that were created when we were six or ten or sixteen. We are adults, and the mental models have to change because the old ones are not serving us now that we are adults.

The subconscious job is to remember and remind that is it. It retains it all, and in doing so, it forms a system that will keep us safe according to what information we have taken in. So, if you were called ugly by a boy, you liked in the fourth grade, and it hurt your feelings and made you feel worthless and unloved this will stick with you. Your subconscious mind will believe that story if you don't change it by knowing that you are beautiful and worthy. You will spend your life picking the wrong men because you don't feel worthy of a healthy relationship. It will keep you safe by not letting you get hurt by the stupid boy in fourth grade again.

In order to change our mental models, we have to start with the conscious mind. Believe you are worthy and intentionally bring positive mental models into your conscious, awake life so it will seep into your subconscious. Once this process has started, you can begin to change the subconscious to a more positive mental model that will serve your life more efficiently. In doing so, your life will start to change dramatically for the better. Here are a few ways to improve it. Practicing these daily will help create a habit that will serve you in a more positive way.

These practices will help, but you don't have to practice all of them. If only a few resonate with you then, only do those few. Do what feels useful to you; if it brings you peace or joy, then that is the ones you need to practice; leave the rest. This practice is supposed to be fun and easy to make into a habit, if you are forcing yourself to do this, then it will be a waste of your time.

Practices for a Positive Mental Model

Be quiet. Take time daily to lie quietly on your back and get in a relaxing state of mind so you can start to visualize a day in your life. Create the day you would love to have happened in your waking life. One option is when you wake for the day, after you come home from work, or right before you go to bed.

Take several, deep breaths and begin to feel your body becoming more relaxed. You want to feel comfortable from your head to your toes. No tension in the body. Once you feel like you are relaxed, then start to visualize your day. Create a perfect day in your mind, what you are eating for breakfast, who are you spending it with, what are you wearing and so on. Be very detailed and consider creating with all your senses. Which means what are you smelling, touching, seeing, tasting, hearing. Feel into it; the more your emotions are involved, the more the subconscious will remember.

The subconscious doesn't know the difference between reality and fantasy; it doesn't know that this day is only happening in your mind, and this is where you start to change your mental models in a more positive way. Try this for 20 minutes a day every day; this is the critical part every day. The more consistent you can become with any practice, the more it will become a habit, and you will retain and continue to practice. Top athletes and high performing people do this in their daily routine; they visualize where they want to be on a regular.

Consider thinking of your perfect day throughout the day. Keep thinking of it. Go to sleep thinking about it. Changes will continue to happen, and before long, you will be living the life you once only created in your mind. Be patient with this process; it will take time for the subconscious to switch to the new mental model, but it will happen.

Believe Change Can Happen for You

Believe change is possible and take action to reflect the new mental model. At first, you may have a hard time believing this new truth because it isn't something you have done before or considered before, BUT it doesn't mean you can't keep trying. It only means you have to keep going and keep telling yourself it is true. Stacey wants to lose 20 pounds by her class reunion in six months. She starts to visualize herself in the dress and how amazing she looks. Not only will she imagine herself being thinner, but she will also take action to make that happen, like working out at the gym daily for 30 minutes, eating a healthy diet and only allowing a few cheats a week. Creating these changes will allow her brain to realize she is serious this time, and the mind will continue to think herself thin.

Permit Yourself to Be Successful

Be happy now, and don't wait until you think you are successful. This one is important to remember. If you keep waiting to be happy you will never be satisfied because what you are telling your subconscious mind is that you have to wait and receive something before you are happy and you aren't happy now. Being happy and grateful now for all that you have and have accomplished will prepare you for when the success comes. When being thankful, you cannot help, but be happy. Thinking of loved ones and experiences you have had will promote positive mental models.

Jordan wanted to be a successful real estate agent. He worked hard and was focused on his goal of earning 60,000 dollars in his first year. He knew he would be happy once the goal has been reached. The goal was met, and Jordan still wasn't happy. He has to be satisfied with what he has right now and yet have new goals set in place to achieve more from himself.

Letting yourself be happy and satisfied currently will only create more positive reinforcement for the future. If you wait to be happy, it will only prolong it. Instead of being content, you will always need the "next big thing" to make you happy. It will be a never-ending cycle that will only keep you unhappy as long as you keep looking to things and success that will only happen in the future. Once the goals have been achieved, recognize them, and celebrate! You have done it. How amazing is that?

Surround Yourself with Positivity

Surround yourself with positive people and things you love. Having people that support what you want to create will help you keep the positive vibe and encourage you to continue when you feel like giving up. Creating space in your house that is just for you and will make you happy when you are in it. Continue to fill your life with things that make you happy and at peace. If all you are doing is working towards your goal and not making time for the people you love and the things you like to do you will inevitably get "burnt out" on all the work and no play.

Put a ritual into place that will encourage play and positive mental models each day, like playing a game for an hour on your phone or watching your favorite tv show, leaving notes on the bathroom mirror telling you how smart and beautiful you are. Again, consistency is the key to succeeding in keeping the balance between working on the goals and keeping yourself sane. Pencil this time in on your busy calendar each day.

Talk About Your Success in Present Form

Remember when I said the subconscious doesn't know the difference between reality and fantasy? That still applies here in speaking as if you HAVE your success now. If you say out loud or in your mind that you ARE successful, your brain will start to believe it. Mental models will be created to think as if you are already successful and are living the life you have always wanted. Having emotions combine with this thinking will only encourage the subconscious to believe it even more.

Another great way to reinforce this belief is by using a mantra. Mantra is a statement that you use to create new positive mental models around the current areas of your life. If you have more month then money, trying to make ends meet and stressing about not having enough money to pay rent, you will only have more lack in your life. If worry starts to make you anxious, take a deep breath, stop the negative pattern, and tell yourself, "My life is full of abundance and money comes easily to me."

Keep telling yourself this mantra until you calm down. Tell yourself this even when you're not stressed. Say it until you really, honestly, believe it. This will take time just like the rest of these practices but, I am telling you the consistency will pay off. Just believe in yourself and your ability to change the way you are thinking. You can create mantras for different areas of your life but, don't make so many it overwhelms you, that would be counter-productive.

Be Crystal Clear on Your Vision

A clear vision of where you are going in life will guide you to take baby steps needed to get to the big goal. If the subconscious has a vague idea like "I want to be rich." There is no direction on how to get there, and a plan can't be put into place to help you get rich. If you explain and have a plan to tell your brain, then it can get excited and be ready to work. It needs direction and emotions to give it fuel to move forward and in the course of getting rich.

Mikah wanted to make a million dollars a year before he is 25 years old. He has a coaching business that he is growing. He has set goals for each year to get him to that million-dollar goal. He is clear in his vision each year and has taken baby steps that will help him get to that goal. Planning and having a clear vision will help you succeed. When you start a road trip across the country, you have a plan, a road map on where to go and know when to stop for gas; it is planned out to get you to your destination. Your life needs that road map to get to the destination as well, and you are in charge of getting that together.

Here is a simple exercise to help you plan for the goal you have set. First, write your goal at the top of a piece of paper (pick only one goal for this.) List all that needs to be done to get you to that goal. These will be "baby steps" to get you to the big goal. Each day work on one step until that step is complete, move on to the next one and so on until you are at the target. Steps may need

to change or even get added but, having a list to start with will help you just start and get active on your dreams. Be grateful along the way, and when the goal is met, don't forget to celebrate the little steps along the way. If you have a small celebration on your way to the big goal, it will give your brain a little reward; this will keep you happy and keep working towards the goal.
Holding conflicting beliefs

This one is a tricky one to figure out; we are saying one thing but, our subconscious is believing and acting on another. We think about taking trips all over the world and doing as we please but, in the back of our minds (subconscious) we are telling ourselves we can't afford to do that. It is hard for humans to think big when the right now seems so small. It is hard to imagine we can have all the riches the world has to offer when we are living in a one-bedroom apartment on the poor side of town. The mind can only see what will be lost if we make a move towards a better life; we don't know what we will gain in the process.

Tabby wants to be a famous singer so bad, but she is afraid to leave her well-paying job to pursue her dream. What she doesn't realize is all that she will gain if she takes this risk. She would no longer have to worry about that job and living to help others with their dreams. She would be free to create and sing every day.

Conflicting beliefs, your conscious mind says yes, but your subconscious says not today. Learn to control the mind and start to create positive mental models to live your best life yet. Practicing these exercises and having a self-care plan will help you overcome the negative subconscious mind and create a subconscious that believes you are capable of doing anything you set your mind too.

Positive Thoughts

Being aware of the negative thought and shutting it down before it has time to get you to stress out and anxious is the path to a more positive lifestyle. Stay aware of the conversation you are having with yourself be conscious of what is going on in your mind. Mistakes will be made; we are human, give yourself a break, and quit beating yourself up of silly stuff that won't matter in five months.

Accept the mistake, apologize if you need too, and let it go. Reliving the error will not make you feel better, and it won't change anything besides you feeling more guilty then you have been in the past. Create mental modes that will serve you and help you let go of stuff that is holding you back. If it doesn't serve you, meaning if it doesn't make your life better or more at peace, then find a way to let it go.

Forgiveness is a great way to let go of the mental models that are conflicting with the new life we want for ourselves. Forgiveness of a person doesn't mean you are letting them "off the hook" with hurting you; it merely means you are moving on and not holding on to all of the hurt that doesn't serve you to be better.

Sandra was engaged to Thomas, and things were going great, she was planning the wedding, and all was well between them. Sandra was so happy and excited to spend the rest of her life with Thomas. One day Thomas texted her and announced he didn't want to marry her and that he was moving to Italy in three weeks. Sandra was devastated, to say the least. She never forgave him and spent the next three years being angry and not dating or seeking another relationship. The anger is holding her back from finding a healthy relationship and enjoying life in general. One day she decided to forgive him, truly bless, and forgive him. After doing this, she felt free; happy and full of life. Forgiveness gave her freedom from the suffering and pain she continued to carry with her.

Any of these practices will change your mental models for more positive ones. Being consistent and recognizing when the negative starts and shutting it down will help mold you into the person you want to be. Mantras will help you stay balanced and confident things will work out in your favor. Forgiving yourself and others will release you from pain and promote happiness and freedom. Set goals and figure out the baby steps needed to help you accomplish that goal. Live a balanced life all work and no play will take a toll on your positive mental models so, be aware of your self-care to keep you balanced.

Chapter 6: Critical Mental Models for Growth

Perception is our experience and interpretation of the world around us. It involves the recognition of external stimuli and the actions in response to the stimuli. We use the perception process to gain knowledge of different systems and their properties. Through perception, we form a relationship with the world around us and learn how to act within it and how to relate to it. Perception is comprised of the detection of stimuli through the five senses, sight, touch, sound, smell and taste. Cognitive processes are required to interpret information and are also involved in the perception process.

Throughout our daily experiences, we are constantly exposed to various stimuli that are present in our environment. We see and observe the systems and objects around us, smell different aromas and hear different sounds. We taste and touch multiple objects continuously in day-to-day life. All these experiences constitute our conscious existence and help define our interactions with the people and systems around us.

Perception typically occurs in 3 steps, these are;

1. Exposure to stimulus or environment.
2. Interpretation of the stimulus.
3. Action in response to the stimulus.

This process occurs naturally and continuously. We live surrounded by stimuli that attract our attention at one point or another. These stimuli include anything that can be touched, heard, seen, tasted, or smelt. The specific stimulus that attracts our attention becomes the attended stimulus. The attended stimulus is transmitted as a neuro signal to the brain. Once it reaches the brain, we then become consciously aware of the presence of the stimulus in the environment. This recognition is then categorized and identified. Once the stimulus has been identified we can then act in an appropriate manner in reaction to the perceived stimulus.

In order to understand and make sense of the world, we take in energy from the environment and convert it to neuro signals; this is the process of sensation. The perception that occurs in a bottom-up sequence of processing begins with the stimulus and ends with the identification and categorization of the stimulus. In top-down processing of perception, the perception is developed based on previous experience and expectations. Information, in this case, is interpreted on the basis of context in which the stimulus occurs or exists. Both types of processes play an important role in perception.

Top-down processing is when we start with a larger object and then acquire more information on the object in question. In top-down processing of perception, we start with a general concept then gradually break it down to more detailed smaller concepts. Top-down processing helps in simplifying our view of the world, by taking in information in broad generalized impressions rather than having to focus on multiple small isolated details. Top-down processing is conceptually driven. It is influenced by expectations, existing beliefs, and our understanding of various systems.

Top-down processing is useful when looking for patterns in the environment but it can confine us to a set and fixed way of perceiving things. We develop a set perception when our experiences and beliefs influence and create a bias in our way of viewing things. The context and circumstances in which an object is perceived can influence our expectations.

Motivation also plays a role in how we see things because we tend to perceive what will reinforce our beliefs. A classic example of top-down processing is evident when reading an article that has typos and spelling errors, we hardly notice them because our brains automatically fill in the blanks and we see the words as they should be and not as they are.

Bottom-up processing in perception differs from top-down processing. In bottom-up processing, perception is purely data-driven and is not influenced by previous knowledge or experience. Bottom-up processing takes place as we interact with the stimuli. Bottom-up processing works on the principle of reductionism by breaking down the system or stimulus into its most basic elements.

As a whole concept perception involves;

- Receiving information.
- Selection of information based on external or internal factors.
- organization of information
- Interpretation of the information.

Perception is a psychological intellectual process that is subjective since individuals can perceive a similar situation in different ways based on their unique experiences and beliefs. Perception plays a big role in the formation of mental models. Mental models are internal representations of our external environment in such a way that we can understand our environment. Mental models are built on how we perceive situations or systems.

Mental models are constructed through perception, imagination, knowledge, and comprehension. Perception influences the kind of mental models we develop and can impair our objectivity since perception is largely subjective and varies from one individual to the next. Over-dependence on set perceptions can restrict our thinking and result in a narrow and incomplete view of the world. To achieve optimum thought processing, we need to have objective views that are not biased or influenced by our past experiences or assumptions.

Mental models can help guide our perception and views of situations. They are the thinking tools that we use to understand life and different systems. They aid us in making decisions, generating new ideas, and solving problems. By organizing and structuring knowledge, mental models simplify concepts it becomes easier to understand complex systems.

Mental models also enable and equip us to understand the links between different systems and how they complement each other's functions and work together. The procedural arrangement of information in mental models enhances our recall function and our ability to re-use skills we utilize frequently with little mental effort.

Decisions and Mental Models

Mental models are comprised of categories of data and knowledge, concepts, identities, stereotypes, casual narratives, and world views. They organize knowledge in a way that we can comprehend, explain, and utilize it. Mental models consolidate knowledge and enable us to process information. Having varied mental models to base our thought processing on is essential for decision making and problem-solving skills.

Life is filled with choices that we need to make daily. These choices range from mundane everyday decisions to life-altering decisions with more far-reaching consequences. Our choices and decisions affect our mental wellbeing, physical health, productivity, and social competence. To make sound decisions we need to be equipped with enough knowledge to base our decisions on, an objective view of the situation and the ability to predict possible outcomes.

Background knowledge and acquired knowledge is necessary for decision making. Without the necessary facts and formation, we cannot assess situations adequately enough to determine the pros and cons of each possible course of action.

The choices we make ultimately have consequences whether in the short or long term. Decisions are therefore an integral factor in determining our success or failure in life. Decisions lead to action, the action leads to a habit which in turn forms a behavior and ultimately a lifestyle.

If we take an example of nutrition, you can either make a conscious decision to maintain a healthy diet or be lax in your nutritional standards. Good nutritional choices will result in good health, reduce your chances of getting lifestyle diseases and enhance your productivity. Poor nutrition, on the other hand, may lead to a negative body image, predisposition to lifestyle diseases and the overall reduction in productivity. In each case, the choice will have an effect on our long-term future.

Emotions can influence us to make decisions that feel good at the moment but that will ultimately affect us adversely in the future. For instance, making a conscious decision to stay in and study instead of going out with friends may not feel good at the moment but may have a positive effect on your educational future.

Mental models allow us to predict the outcome of our decisions through mental simulations. Simulations involve running different scenarios through your mind and determining what would be the likely outcome of each. Based on the desired outcome we can then settle on the scenario that leads us closest to our goals.

Past experience helps us to learn from the consequences of past mistakes and guides us on the courses of action to avoid if we are to have better experiences in the future. For instance, if your business went under due to mismanagement of funds in the past, you are likely to be more cautious in future ventures when managing your funds since you have already experienced the consequences of mismanagement.

Mental models organize and structure information into processes based on our experiences and knowledge, hence using them can help in avoiding pitfalls that we suffered in the past.

Our decisions affect not only us but also those around us. Effective managers and leaders are aware of this fact and take other people's needs, concerns and values into consideration while making decisions. Leadership and management positions carry the added responsibility of ensuring that the decisions made are beneficial for all the people involved. It is important to consider the following when making decisions:

- Decisions have consequences both in the short term and long term.
- Decisions are influential and can impact on others and on our environments.
- Decisions are an illustration of our values, beliefs, and character.

Mental models such as probabilistic thinking are important in the decision-making process. Outcomes are determined by a complex set of factors that shape the outcome of any particular scenario. Probabilistic thinking helps us determine what our choices are likely to lead to and the alternative courses of action available to us to achieve the desired outcome. Using probabilistic thinking as a mental model can help us to anticipate what is likely to happen and in so doing, we can be prepared for the eventuality.

The inversion model of thinking is also a useful model that can have a significant role in enhancing our decision-making process. By enabling us to tackle a situation from the end rather than the beginning, it makes it easier to identify the obstacles blocking our path to achievement of the desired goal. Inversion gives us the opportunity to view a problem from perspectives, the beginning as well as the end.

When you have the ultimate goal, you are pursuing in the front of your mind, it becomes easy to work backward and do everything in your power to achieve the goal that you have visualized. While inverting the situation does not automatically imply that the problem will be solved, it does help in identifying obstacles in our paths and avoiding them.

When trying to make a decision we are often overwhelmed by information and trying to figure out the best course of action. Applying the first principles of thinking mental model helps us to clarify complicated situations by separating facts from assumptions and leaving the basics of the situations. You can then build new knowledge around the basics and arrive at a new conclusion or solution to the problem.

We all have mental models that serve as our framework for understanding the world around us. Mental models shape our behavior and thought processes equipping us to solve problems, identify opportunities, generate ideas, and make sound decisions. Filtering information through mental models gives us a better comprehension of a system and how it works.

Mental models are formed on the basis of our perception, experience, and acquired knowledge. Mental models can generally be characterized as:

- Dynamic and constantly evolving with experience and acquisition of knowledge
- Incomplete representations of reality based on individual perception.
- They provide simplified explanations of complex phenomena
- They are the basic structures of cognition.

Our reasoning is based on mental models. These models represent a perception or view of external stimuli. Mental models will typically depict possibilities and can be used to predict outcomes through mental simulation. Mental models have an organized structure in long term memory. They also contain declarative information, causal information about how components of a system interact and procedural information about how to operate the system to achieve the desired outcome.

Mental model structures are typically organized as a network with information bits that are interlinked representing interconnected concepts of a larger system. The structure of the mental model provides the foundation for behavior to be established. Mental models are predictive in nature and create simulations that arise from the underlying knowledge and information contained in the structure of the model. These simulations give possible outcomes based on possible scenarios. Organized knowledge is easier to recall and put to use hence mental models also facilitate recollection of information.

Construction of a mental model normally occurs in stages,

- Identifying the components of a system.
- Inter grating the components of the system based on their interactions
- Testing and running the model.

Mental model structure development has been found to differ based on the level of experience. In highly experienced individuals, there is a high level of linkages within the networks that make up the mental model. Subnetworks are also common in highly experienced individuals' mental models. The level of abstraction in these mental models is also higher with associations and a concept is based on abstract information rather than surface features as is the case in amateurs or individuals with little experience.

In individuals with more experience, sub-groupings and interactions are based on frequently used procedures. When it comes to language, the associations are based on the meaning of words in the context of the domain of the system. The structure in amateur individuals' mental models differs from the structure in the models of experts or highly experienced individuals. The models in this group have a lower level of abstraction with concepts being based on surface characteristics rather than abstract concepts.

The mental models in amateurs have fewer interlinkages between concepts and the networks within the model are not as dense as those in the mental models of experts.

The language used is also a key difference between the structures of the two types of mental models. In amateurs, the meaning of words is based on natural language rather than the language of the system in question. In these mental models, the concepts are not arranged in a procedural format unlike in the mental models of people with more experience.

The principle of accumulating mental models is instrumental in improving our thinking capacity and our ability to see situations from multiple perspectives. When we rely on a fixed number or set of mental models, we in effect limit our range of thought, our capacity to generate new ideas and the aptitude for finding solutions to problems. To improve ourselves we must first change the way we think and how our thoughts influence our actions. This is only possible if we are willing to expand our set of mental models.

By considering mental models as tools that we can use to facilitate effective thinking we can comprehend that the more mental models we have at our disposal, the better the decisions we are able to make and to best utilize our knowledge when interacting with different systems.

Our attitudes, values, beliefs, actions, and behavior are shaped by our thoughts. To achieve something, we must first conceive it in our minds before we can bring it into reality. The importance of mental models can thus not be stressed enough. Not only do they affect our personal growth and development, but they also influence our interactions and experiences with others and our effectiveness at the workplace and in other intellectual pursuits.

Looking at the world through the perspective of one subject or body of knowledge leads to a limited and biased perception of the world and limits our ability to adapt our thoughts to reflect reality. Our education system mainly focuses on creating experts in specific bodies of knowledge such as biology, physics, geology, and many other specialist disciplines. To be exemplary thinkers, we must be willing to break out of the mold of our fields of expertise and pursue liquid knowledge. Liquid knowledge is the knowledge that encompasses multiple fields and has utility across various situations in day-to-day life.

Liquid knowledge facilitates the formation of interlinked concepts within the mental model. It forms co-relationships between related concepts establishing similarities and areas of interactions across different fields of knowledge and expertise. These linkages within the mental model are important in creating opportunities and innovative ideas that would otherwise be missed if we limited ourselves to just one area of expertise. Mastering the fundamentals of each discipline will open up your view of the world and enable you to perceive situations from multiple points of view and enhance your understanding of the world.

Organizations can also benefit from the construction and development of shared mental models. Shared mental models create a common understanding of tasks to be undertaken, foster effective teamwork and create an organizational culture. When people establish common objectives, shared perception, and similar motivations they are able to work harmoniously in teams to aid in the achievement of common goals.

Shared mental models are used to define, explain, and predict the behavior of teams. It is not possible to have different individuals having identical mental models, it is, however, possible for their mental models to be compatible in terms of major perceptions and in their system of processing knowledge and information. Identifying and fostering compatible models among team members is the primary objective of developing shared mental models.

Having compatible mental models means that the team members have a common understanding of how the task ahead needs to be tackled, their individual roles in the accomplishment of the task and how to connect their roles and functions to create a functional unit.

Knowledge stability is an important part of the shared mental model framework. Understanding the role of each individual within the team will create a clearly defined course of action based on the identified roles of each individual and what each member should be doing to complement the other member's efforts. For instance, if paramedics are called out to an emergency situation, understanding the role of each team member will help to ensure there are no gaps in their response procedures and this will in effect help to determine where to best position each person in the response team to enhance team effort and effectiveness. Ambiguity within the team in terms of individual roles and functions can result in duplication of functions or some areas of the task being ignored since team members do not have information on each other's functions.

Effective teams can use shared mental models to predict and simulate possible outcomes using different scenarios. The predictive aspect of mental models is important in identifying possible challenges that may affect the achievement of objectives and in determining ways to overcome them. This will as a result help in planning and preparation for the expected outcome. The ability to anticipate problems and areas of weakness means that team members are equipped to assist each other and function in harmony in different situations to enhance their collective effectiveness.

Shared mental models help teams by;

- Creating a mutual understanding of a situation or task.
- Establishing effective communication among team members.
- Create an understanding of the individual and each other's roles within the team and how these roles intersect to facilitate the completion of the task.
- Enable anticipation of team needs and prediction of possible outcomes

- Create unified goals and purposes.

For shared mental models to be effective they must provide an accurate representation of reality. A realistic picture is important in creating a viable plan of action. Without having an accurate picture of reality, it is impossible to come up with an effective plan since the starting point is not based on the actual situation. The shared mental model should unite and align the goals and visions of the individual to those of the company.

At both personal and organizational levels, the necessity of mental models for effective decision making and better thought processes cannot be ignored. Training your brain to think in new ways will enable you to tackle problems that you could not solve before, see opportunities that were previously hidden and have an unbiased multi-disciplinary view of systems and the world at large.

The structure of mental models is comprised of acquired knowledge and pre-existing knowledge or past experiences. The creation of linkages between these major facets enables inferences to be drawn from past experience and these inferences are used to interpret the current situations we find ourselves in. Experience is, therefore, one of the core components in the formation and development of mental models.

Mental models are our tools for understanding and explaining situations and systems. Mental models are also predictive in nature. They allow for predictions of outcomes through mental simulations. By creating simplified internal representations of complex external situations, mental models enhance our understanding of complex situations and enhance our thought processes by structuring and organizing knowledge in a manner that is easy to understand and recall.

Mental models are agents of behavior change. By affecting how we think they ultimately influence our actions and behavior. They affect how we think through the following mechanisms:

- Organizing background information into simpler concepts
- Creating reference points from past experience and memory.
- Linking information and facts.
- Enabling mental simulations that aid in predicting possible outcomes and in anticipation of future events.

Critical Models to Include in Your Set of Cognitive Models

Logic and reason are the main source and measures of knowledge. It allows a person to discover the systems around them and interpret them in a rational way. The theory of rationalism stipulates that people rely on experiences and intuition to form perceptions of various systems. Our cognitive aptitude is mainly important in decision making, problem-solving and also idea generation.

The nature of human psychology is to alter our reality to fit our beliefs and mental models. If you rely on a few models your perception will always be skewed to accommodate them and this will hinder your objectivity and ability to see situations from multiple perspectives.

Multiple models are a necessary element for personal growth. However, it is not enough to have multiple models but the models should also be from multiple disciplines because everybody of knowledge or discipline consists of knowledge that we need to be aware of if we are to have a comprehensive and realistic view of the world. Multi-disciplinary mental models enhance your cognitive aptitude and the ability to make intelligent and strategic decisions.

It is important to understand your cognitive limitations in order to be more open to alternative approaches and the adoption of creative methodologies. In this regard, self-awareness becomes a great tool because we can only seek to improve once we know what our strengths and weaknesses are. Establishing your personal competencies and being acutely aware of the areas in which you are likely to excel and those in which you fall short will aid you in identifying the mental models you need to adopt to enhance your cognitive aptitude.

There are many different mental models in different fields of knowledge. These mental models range in complexity from basic common-sense models to complex and sophisticated models. Creating a latticework of both the simple and complex models will give an understanding of straight forward concepts but also help you to interpret and breakdown complex systems into component concepts that you can understand and recall.

Some of the models that can enhance your cognitive ability and reasoning are;

Entropy

The principle of entropy is multi-disciplinary. There is entropy in physics, statistics, information theory, and cosmic studies. Entropy by definition is a measure of chaos or disorder. It can also be used to refer to changes in systems. Low entropy implies that the level of randomness is low within a system, on the flip side high entropy implies a high level of randomness in a system.

We increase entropy by increasing the complexity of the knowledge we have. Entropy is bound to increase over time with advances in technology and various other innovations. To control entropy in the systems around us we have to focus on the aspect that we can control.

The law of entropy is built upon the principle of devoting energy resources and time to the things that we have control over and have the capacity to change. Trying to exert control on circumstances beyond our control is not only an exercise in futility but a waste of energy, time and resources that could be better utilized elsewhere.

Small restorations of order in our lives such as organizing your desk at work or cleaning your room can have a tangible effect in creating the sense that you are restoring order in your life. An ordered and clean-living environment results in an ordered mind and even small acts of restoring order and control can go a long way in making us feel like we are in control of ourselves and the environment in which we exist.

The best way to internalize this model is to start small with small tasks such as organizing your closet, cleaning your house, or even organizing your desk at work. These may seem like small acts but they are surprisingly effective in creating a sense of orderliness around us and minimizing the feeling of being in a chaotic environment.

Pavlovian Association

The Pavlovian association principle is a great model for self-awareness and social awareness. Self-awareness is the ability to recognize and understand our emotions, while social awareness is the ability to understand and manage the emotions of those around us.

Pavlovian association refers to the conditioning of the mind to form associations between objects. For instance, ringing the bell every time you feed the dog will teach the dog to associate the bell with food. This means that the bell will elicit the same reaction as the food would even when the dog is not being fed.

The Pavlovian association is used both consciously and unconsciously. Most of the associations are created at a subconscious level and are therefore almost impossible to resist since we may not even be aware that the association is happening. This model is crucial in building self-awareness because it can unearth the reactions we have based on mere association rather than actual reality. Similarly figuring out when other people are reacting based on association alone can help us in understanding their emotions and consequently increase the ability to persuade and influence them.

The Why Model

The power of why lies in the ability to make us question our actions, beliefs, and values. When we self-analyze by prodding our inner motivations, we can establish concrete plans and courses of action that will help us in reaching our goals and objectives. The power of why requires us to justify our own actions and this can help in detecting destructive habits and consequently in changing behavior in a positive manner.

The power of why is also widely applied in leadership to motivate the masses to action and create a common analogy and sense of purpose. The justification aspect of the why models lead to crystallized reasoning which means we obtain a sense of purpose and direction.

The why a model principle is a powerful tool when it is used in business strategy especially in the sales function. By asking the right questions a salesman can establish a need for a product in the client. Through justification, he can illustrate why the product is necessary and this will go a long way in making his pitch effective.

The why the model principle is also important in achieving effective communication of information and knowledge. Regardless of how complex a situation or system is if you explain it from the point of view of why? People are more likely to understand the concept faster. When we know the reason behind something then it becomes easier to build the rest of the knowledge about the system around that justification.

This mental model helps us determine and understand motivation, intentions, objectives, and expected outcomes. It is useful in decision making, planning, and creating a strong sense of purpose and direction.

Bias from over Influence by Authority

Throughout history, social organization has divided people into rulers and subjects. Bias from over influence by authority is inculcated from a young age. We are taught to respect and obey authority figures as a way of maintaining order in society. Authority gives people a sense of security arising from the sense that there is someone in control.

By having the ability to question authority we can keen excessive power and the abuse of this power in check. Dictators over time have been known to commit grievous atrocities because they commanded absolute power and authority over their subject. Authority like any other responsibility and privilege needs to have checks and balances to keep it within the boundaries of reason and political correctness.

Inversion Model

Thinking backward is more effective in tackling a problem because it deconstructs a situation making simple concepts out of a complex situation. Thinking backward helps us in recognizing the obstacles that are between us and our goals and with this knowledge we can work on eliminating them.

Inversion is also effective because in breaking down complex situations into smaller bits the situation becomes less overwhelming and easier to understand. We can address the situation concept by concept instead of looking at a problem as an insurmountable mountain.

Inversion also clarifies the consequences of a specific course of action and these not only help in picking the best scenario for the desired outcome but also helps in handling stress and anxiety that comes with the fear of the unknown. When you are able to anticipate what will happen you are more likely to remain calm since you are prepared mentally for what is to come.

Circle of Competence

Self-awareness is crucial in identifying our level of personal competence. Being self-aware enables us to determine what we are gifted in, where we have shortcomings and need to improve and what motivates us. These are the key ingredients that facilitate personal growth and development. By understanding our weaknesses, we can alter the habits and thoughts that lead us to destructive behavior. In so doing we will be able to consistently improve ourselves and take maximum advantage of our strengths.

Establishing what your circle of competence is, improves our decision-making process by eliminating ego-driven choices. Every human being is flawed in one way or another, being self-aware helps us in setting realistic objectives for ourselves and keeping our weaknesses in check. Over-reaching for what is naturally beyond our capabilities may lead to constant failure which would ultimately impact our self-confidence and in turn reduce our motivation.

Basing our objectives on a realistic assessment of our abilities means that we can set achievable goals and objectives and focus our energy on building on our strengths and compensating for our weaknesses.

Models to Adopt for Better Thought and Decision Making

Life is essentially a series of choices that we make to determine the direction in which we need our life to follow. From mundane everyday decisions to complex life-altering decisions we face choices on a daily basis. Choices have consequences and every decision we make will have a consequence. The quality of decisions we make will determine if they result in adverse consequences or have a positive outcome.

Decisions not only affect us but also those that we interact with and have relationships with and our external environment as a whole. We, therefore, need to take into consideration the needs and concerns of others before making decisions. To avoid making knee jerk decisions based on emotions and opinions it's critical that we have a sound thought process through which we can filter information before arriving at a decision.

Our thoughts not only influence our actions but also shape our beliefs, attitudes, opinions, and behavior. It is therefore important to recognize that our thoughts essential shape and influence all aspects of our lives. We should thus make conscious and consistent effort to improve our thought processes to enable us to make better decisions and cope with the ever-changing world that we live in.

Mental models are the lens through which we view the world and filter information to better comprehend systems and the situations around us. Developing these models is crucial in creating more efficient thought processes that combine knowledge and experience to form comprehensive interpretations of complex systems and enhance our understanding of concepts and information. This ability to understand, comprehend and utilize knowledge forms the basis through which we can make informed choices and sound decisions.

To develop a wide understanding of the world we need to draw knowledge from varied and multi-disciplinary models that address multiple aspects of different systems. These multiple models will give us fluid knowledge that does not just give us give us the expertise in a selected field but rather knowledge we can utilize in multiple situations.

Some of the models we can use to expand and enhance our decision-making process include;

Adaptation

To thrive in their habitat's species must adapt to their ever-changing ecosystem or die. The process of natural selection eliminates the weaker species and leaves the stronger ones to survive and breed. This ensures that future generations carry the best genes from the available gene pool. Natural selection is a basic law of biology where nature lets the strong survive and eliminates the weak. This is nature's way of guaranteeing the survival of a species by systemically getting rid of undesirable characteristics in the gene pool.

The law of adaptation holds true across all facets of life. It is as important in human existence as it is in species survival in the wild. The world constantly changing and evolving and if we fail to keep up with the changes in technology, climate, socials set up and all the other spheres of life we risk being rendered redundant. Adaptability is what equips us to handle change and process new information and figure out how to respond to it. We cannot achieve adaptability without being open to new ways of thinking. We cannot successfully apply old ways of thinking to new situations and expect success. Our thoughts must keep in tune with the changing world to enable us to face new challenges, generate new ideas and find solutions to modern problems.

Adding this model to your set of mental models will enhance your personal growth and capacity for innovation. New ways of reasoning and yield new ideas which intern lead to innovation and the discovery of new ideas.

Mental Simulations

One of the key elements of mental models is the ability to predict future outcomes. Using acquired knowledge and experience we anticipate possible outcomes through mental simulations. In decision making it is crucial to be able to anticipate the consequences of whichever action we choose to undertake. This will help us in picking the choice whose consequences are equal to or closest to our objectives.

Mental simulations aid us in predicting the possible outcomes of our actions. These predictions can be employed in determining the best course of action to use to achieve the desired outcome. When we walk through different scenarios in our minds, we get a realistic insight into what might occur and how it may affect us. This ability to anticipate future events helps us prepare for the outcome and also change our course of action to avoid undesirable outcomes.

Pareto's Principle

When making decisions, it is crucial to understand how best to spend our resources energy and time. Time management is an essential element in increasing productivity and managing resources effectively. Pareto's principle enables us to determine the activities that yield the highest results and in effect spend more time and energy on them instead of devoting time to non-productive ventures.

This principle stipulates that results are not equally distributed. It's been established that 20% of the work typically generates 80% of the results. This is evident in fields such as sales where from a portfolio of clients, you are likely to secure the most business from a small percentage (20%) of the group. This knowledge is important in directing us on how to spend our time and energy on the most productive aspects while devoting minimal attention to the least productive aspects.

Making a choice based on this principle will save you the trouble of pursuing fruitless endeavors that may end up being a drain on time and resources.

First-Principles of Thought

By understanding the first elements and basic principles of a system, we can build factual knowledge around the main principles and eliminate assumptions that infiltrate our decision-making process. Assumptions are usually based on emotional reactions and individual biases hence when we make assumption-based decisions the fact tends to get mixed up with perceptions and biases that create a distorted view of reality.

By comprehending the first principles of a system we create a factual knowledge base that we can then use as a realistic and sound basis on which to build our knowledge on and make inferences.

Decisions based on facts are more likely to reflect the true reality of the situation we seek to address. This principle eliminates bias and assumptions that can cloud our judgment when deciding which choice is best for achieving our intended objectives.

Bayesian Method

One of the key determinants of the appropriate course of action to take is the expected result or consequence of the choice that will be made. Thinking ahead to see the implication of a choice we make today will have in the future is perhaps the easiest way to determine which choices are feasible and which should be ruled out from consideration.

The Bayesian method is a thought process where one considers all probable outcomes and scenarios. By adding new information onto the prior knowledge gained from experiences and updating them, we create a more realistic expectation and can thus make decisions based on the most likely outcomes. This method is important because we live in a dynamic world that changes from one day to the next. By constantly updating our field of probabilities we can create more realistic simulations on which we can base our decisions.

Occam's Razor

The principle of Occam's razor is concerned with simplicity as opposed to complex situations. It encourages us to focus on simple solutions to problems before contemplating complex interpretations. When we start with the simple concepts, we can systematically work our way up to the complex building our knowledge and cognitive abilities along the way.

This law stipulates that the simplest explanation is often correct. Spending time and energy contemplating complex scenarios may be counterproductive and frustrating. Basing decisions on simpler logic and scenarios creates self-confidence by limiting self-doubt and encouraging one to trust their first instincts. This is the general principle of Occam's razor.

Hanlon's Razor

It is human nature to try and assign blame when things go wrong. Unfortunately, this way of thinking does not create a solution but results in needless aggravation and conflicts. By choosing to focus on what will help us achieve our goals instead and avoiding distractions we are bound to be more focused and purpose-driven.

The principle of Hanlon's razor is mainly a system of thinking that involves the focus of thoughts on solutions rather than finding fault. In this school of thought, bad situations are not attributed to malice or evil intentions but rather to lack of knowledge. When we waste time in paranoid pursuit of people or situations to blame for our circumstances, we might miss opportunities by focusing on the non-productive aspect of a situation. Focusing on finding a solution renders fault-finding irrelevant as we concentrate on fixing the issue not finding its cause.

Reciprocity

This law is based on a principle in physics that stipulates that for every action there is an equal and opposite reaction. This is a multi-disciplinary law that applies not only in physics but also in biology, human behavior, and many other fields. We can use this law to comprehend the consequences of our actions and behavior.

The law of reciprocity is perhaps one of the most important laws to employ in decision making. The understanding that our decisions will undoubtedly have consequences in the short, as well as long term, should always be at the back of our minds when we are making a choice. This knowledge will help us in making responsible and logical choices and ensures that we are prepared to face the consequences of those decisions.

Relativity

The law of relativity originates from the field of physics but has wide utility across different spheres of life. This theory has multiple uses in different contexts in physics. The most widely used concept from this law, however, is the fact that an individual is incapable of fully comprehending a system of which they are part. In physics, a person in a boat may not physically feel the motion of the boat but an observer can observe the movement that is occurring. Similarly, in social situations when a person is in the middle of an experience or situation, they cannot judge it from an objective perspective.

This principle encourages us to assess situations by using an observer's perspective or considering it from the other person's perspective. We are bound to be biased if we have to make a decision that will affect us directly. To be truly objective and realistic in our perception we must first put some physical and mental distance between us and the situation to achieve some level of neutrality. Making decisions from a position that is biased is likely to impact negatively on the course of action that we take.

Catalysts

A catalyst is a substance that speeds up a chemical reaction but remains separate from the reaction itself. These can be found in social situations as well as in science. Identifying catalysts in normal day-to-day life can alter the course of our achievements and the rate at which we achieve them.

When making decisions we should be able to incorporate factors that will enhance our progress and push us further in the direction we need to go in. In life, it's always easy to support and guidance in others. This guidance can help us in avoiding pitfalls and in picking up best practice strategies that have helped our peers achieve the same goals that we are also in pursuit of.

Leverage

The law leverage is concerned with finding ways to make complex situations simple. By employing tools and aids either physically or mentally we can simplify seemingly complex situations and make them easier to process, understand and solve.

Many innovations in engineering have been based on the principle of leverage. Leverage lightens otherwise heavy loads and makes work easier. The ability to find leverage in day-to-day life situations is a major contributor to success. By helping us conserve energy and resources we can devote the saved energy to other areas and accomplish more than when we devote all our actions to only one particular task.

Inertia

Inertia is a basic physical principle that is related to motion. Inertia minimizes energy use by limiting motion and action. This is common in the human condition when we allow ourselves to be moved forward by circumstances rather than concerted personal effort.

Inertia sets in when we feel that we have no control over our circumstance so we just end up riding the wave and letting it deliver us where it will. This can be a dangerous way of thinking because we lose control of our actions and behaviors by letting external forces dictate our course of action and what happens to us a result. We should always strive to exercise some level of control over the situations in our lives and take responsibility for what happens to us by actively making decisions that are in line with our goals and objectives.

Conclusion

Thanks for making it through to the end of *Mental Models Tools*, let's hope it was informative and able to provide you with all of the tools you need to achieve your goals, whatever it is that they may be. Just because you've finished this book doesn't mean there is nothing left to learn on the topic, and expanding your horizons is the only way to find the mastery you seek.

Now that you have made it to the end of this book, you hopefully have an understanding of how to get started building new mental models, as well as a strategy or two, or three, that you are anxious to try for the first time. Before you go ahead and start giving it your all, however, it is important that you have realistic expectations as to the level of success you should expect in the near future.

While it is perfectly true that some people experience serious success right out of the gate, it is an unfortunate fact of life that they are the exception rather than the rule. What this means is that you should expect to experience something of a learning curve, especially when you are first figuring out what works for you. This is perfectly normal, however, and if you persevere you will come out the other side better because of it. Instead of getting your hopes up to an unrealistic degree, you should think of your time spent improving your mental models as a marathon rather than a sprint which means that slow and steady will win the race every single time.

www.ingramcontent.com/pod-product-compliance
Lightning Source LLC
Chambersburg PA
CBHW070703250726
48662CB00001B/231